. . . .

FAMILY OF EARTH

. . . .

FAMILY *of* EARTH

....

A SOUTHERN MOUNTAIN CHILDHOOD

....

Wilma Dykeman

FOREWORD BY ROBERT MORGAN

THE

UNIVERSITY OF

NORTH CAROLINA

PRESS

Chapel Hill

This book was published with the assistance of the William R. Kenan Jr. Fund of the University of North Carolina Press.

Manufactured in the United States of America

Designed by Richard Hendel

Set in Utopia and Bodoni Oldstyle

by codeMantra, Inc.

The University of North Carolina Press has been a member of the Green Press Initiative since 2003.

Cover illustration: Wilma Dykeman and her father on the back steps of her birthplace, about 1922. Photograph courtesy of Jim Stokely.

Library of Congress Cataloging-in-Publication Data

Names: Dykeman, Wilma, author. | Morgan, Robert, 1944– writer of foreword.

Title: Family of earth : a Southern mountain childhood / Wilma Dykeman.

Description: Chapel Hill : The University of North Carolina Press, [2016]

Identifiers: LCCN 2015049261 | ISBN 9781469630540 (cloth : alk. paper) | ISBN 9781469629148 (pbk : alk. paper) | ISBN 9781469629155 (ebook)

Subjects: LCSH: Dykeman, Wilma. | Authors, American— North Carolina—Biography.

Classification: LCC PS3554.Y5 Z46 2016 | DDC 813/.54—dc23

LC record available at http://lccn.loc.gov/2015049261

. . . .
CONTENTS
. . . .

A section of photographs begins on page 63

FOREWORD

AFTER WILMA DYKEMAN'S DEATH in December 2006, her son, James Stokely III, searching through papers in her house in Newport, Tennessee, found a box labeled "Northwestern." Under material relating to Dykeman's graduation from Northwestern University in 1940, he discovered a two-hundred-page memoir which the author had either lost or forgotten. It would appear the manuscript was written during World War II, when the author was in her early to mid twenties, probably after the return to her native Asheville, North Carolina. This memoir, *Family of Earth*, adds significantly to her legacy of fiction and nonfiction. It is clear that from the first Dykeman was a very accomplished writer.

Wilma Dykeman (May 1920–December 2006) belonged to a second generation of gifted Southern and Southern Appalachian writers, following the literary renaissance of Faulkner, Thomas Wolfe, Eudora Welty, James Still, Margaret Mitchell, Erskine Caldwell, among others. Along with Mary Lee Settle, Harriette Arnow, John Ehle, she furthered and deepened the literary heritage of the Southern Appalachian region. In both fiction and nonfiction, in workshops, lectures, classes at the University of Tennessee, in reviews and newspaper columns, she enriched the cultural life of the region for half a century. And with her husband, James Stokely Jr., she played a significant part in the discussion of the social, environmental, and racial issues of her time.

For those of us who have known Dykeman's work for decades, and for those just discovering her fiction and nonfiction, the memoir *Family of Earth* is a treasure. Here we encounter an unusually gifted and observant young writer, exploring her voice, meditating with eloquence and lyrical passion on her life and family and the world from which she came. The writing is alive, with a fresh sense of wonder. The detail is intimate, sensuous, sometimes cinematic. In this memoir there is a special sense of thresholds connecting the past, the traditional, with the modern present.

The two themes that stand out in the memoir are the closeness to the natural world of trees, streams, butterflies, flowers, and the progress of the seasons and the closeness to family and a great variety of other people, including Aunt Maude, the Preacher, Old Man Milligan. As the author says on page 10, "The life of one human is the life of every other living thing on earth."

It is thrilling to watch the young Dykeman explore the "fresh papyrus of memory" (11). The narrative reveals an unusually intense recall of infancy, the discovery of the self as a "triumph of lone splendor" (16). The truth is Wilma Dykeman was a poet as well as a prose writer, evoking the rumble of stones in a flooded stream, moments of hush, the many varieties of wildflowers, the "Aladdin's lantern" (38) of childhood imagination, the death in nature that feeds life, the beauty of forest fires, butter making, tent caterpillars, dirt-daubers and katydids, hounds baying on the mountain, a rooster crowing in the middle of the night.

On page 37 Dykeman says, "I do not believe that any true realist . . . can help being a romantic." Yet for all the romance and magic in her memories, there is a great deal of realism also as she recounts the pain of the Land Boom collapse in Asheville and the Great Depression, the "leanness" of mountain children, the loss of childhood imagination, the hurt of missed connections with those we know and love. The portrait of her father and the account of his illness and death are especially poignant.

In this early work Dykeman does not turn away from the tragic, the harsh, the essential loneliness of the human condition. She admits to a sense of not fitting in, either in the mountain community or in the society of Asheville, caught somewhere between two worlds and not belonging wholly to either. At dance lessons she feels like an intruder. Her social conscience is awakened when she realizes that sometimes when one gained, "somebody, somewhere paid a price" (98).

On page 95 Dykeman writes, "I had no talent for boredom," which can serve as the theme of this memoir and all her writing. This long-lost book is her testimony of "tast[ing] the fire" (118) of poetry and the world around her. She speaks of an infinite curiosity for history, biography, for gardening and the rhythms and routines of the natural world, for travel, for exploration of solitude, for the "singularity of my home-life" (80). Her words serve as both telescope and microscope, making the distant in time close, enlarging the minute fact until it is luminous.

MY FIRST ENCOUNTER with the writing of Wilma Dykeman was with her nonfiction classic *The French Broad*. Reading that book was an important event in my discovery of the history of the Southern Appalachian region. *The French Broad* is such a vivid book and such a loving book, packed with information and insight, memorable writing, environmental consciousness. It gives us a living sense of the land, the watershed of the French Broad, the geology and geography, the Cherokee Indians, and the development of the culture of the area.

If I had to choose one image from *The French Broad* (New York: Holt, Rinehart and Winston, 1955) to illustrate what inspired me most, it would be the motif of springs. Dykeman's description of the headsprings of the river, and the importance of springs to the people, thrilled me and helped me remember much about my own family's spring. I had grown up drinking from and looking into springs: "The cold sweet springs of these mountains . . . which feed with thousands of steady streams to make a river, have been valued for generations by the families they feed. If halfway up a hillside or deep in the heart of some remote cove you see a house and wonder why its people built there rather than on easier slopes, the answer is probably their water. Cupped in a clear steady pool under a thicket of blackberry vines and old shade trees, their spring bubbles from the earth like a rare gift for the taking" (11–12).

A little later, when I read her fiction, I made equally significant discoveries about Western North Carolina and about writing. I saw that the inevitable focus of fiction about the region was on the land and the seasons, and the strong women who struggled on the land to raise children and feed large families, to keep families together over the generations, through wars and natural disasters, sickness and poverty. There could be no better model for a young writer than Dykeman's first novel, *The Tall Woman* (New York: Holt, Rinehart and Winston, 1962). Lydia Moore McQueen is the glue and the inspiration that hold her family and community together across the years of war, sickness, outliers, greed, disappointment, and prejudice. Lydia is very much an individual, but also a personification of the culture at its best. And her interest in springs, and the loving description of springs, are among the most memorable passages in the novel. On pages 176–77 the spring on her property is described in passionate detail:

> "And what are you doing on this bleak day on this godforsaken mountain?" Dr. Hornsby asked.
>
> She laughed at the gloom of his words, belied in part by the heartiness of his smile. "Cleaning my spring."
>
> "And pray tell me, Lydia McQueen," he said, "how do you clean a spring? Do you wash the water?"
>
> "Don't be making fun of me! There"—she pointed with the hoe—"look under the ledge where the roots of those poplar trees are, and tell me if you ever set eyes on a bolder, finer spring than this? Or a cleaner one?"
>
> He went and looked. The natural bowl of water, surrounded on three sides and overhead by a ledge of rock and tangled web of roots and earth, stood clear and cold as glass. Around the spring and beside the stream that flowed from it were beds

of moss and galax, a luxuriant winter green, and the vines of other carefully preserved plants that bloomed in summer. On the far side and overhanging the spring, were a dozen wild blackberry stalks. There were no other briers or dead weeds or fallen limbs around the spot. Someone had worked here lovingly and well.

"I've never set eyes on a bolder, finer spring," he repeated. "Or a cleaner one." "This is my favorite place on our farm," she said.

Water is an important theme in Dykeman's second novel, *The Far Family* (New York: Holt, Rinehart and Winston, 1966), as well.

"One thing about this jumping-off-place your sawmilling dragged us to, Tom Thurston," Aunt Tildy said, "it's got as good water as ever I tasted."

"Now that's a fact," Tom agreed, pleased.

"Only better water I know of anywhere," Martha said quietly, "is the spring on Grandpa Moore's farm." (52)

This second novel follows the heirs of Lydia Moore McQueen far beyond the small farms in the mountains. It is a novel of growth, development, education, politics, finance, and power, as Dykeman tells the story of this particular family in the twentieth-century mountains and beyond. It is a story of family dynamics, of loyalty and conflict, betrayal and sacrifice. Two generations later Ivy visits the Moore homestead and feels the bond of blood and kinship across time:

Two stone steps surrounded by moss and ferns and tiny wild flowers led down to the natural bowl of water, scooped deep in the sparkling sand, chilled by the secret depths from which it flowed. The spring's overflow ran under a stone slab into the springhouse where a long wooden trough held crocks, pitchers of milk, pans of butter in the cool constant stream of water. . . .

There was more than land and buildings to the farm, however. There was a past, the presence of those who had turned this ground before, swept these floors and cleaned this springhouse during many yesterdays. Ivy had never before been part of this feeling of aged places, familiar paths. Her mother involved them in this sense of continuity and the children were captivated. (104)

In this second novel, as in *The French Broad* and *The Tall Woman*, Dykeman shows a considerable knowledge and affection for rural mountain life. She demonstrates how much the sense of who we are comes from memory. But she also reveals an equally acute understanding of modern city life, of the worlds of business, politics, affluent families. There is a knowing satiric edge to her portraits of country clubs and cocktail parties, the chemistry of political events, romance among the upper classes. In *The Far Family* she takes us from Jesse Moore's springhouse to the champagne at a country club bash three generations later.

Phil Cortland, the young senator and descendant of Lydia McQueen, returns to his hometown at a moment of family crisis, and attends a dinner party with his old flame Sherry: "Phil talked with them all, effortlessly using the attentive interest in other people which was his greatest political asset. There were the middle-aged young, the middle-aged old, natives and newcomers, the pleasantly wined and dined and the outright drunk, the ones on the way up, the ones on the way down, and those who were holding on. The chief fact that struck him about them was how much alike they were" (311).

One of the themes Dykeman dramatizes in *The Far Family* is the standardization of modern life. With the coming of roads and railroads, mass communication, outside investment and industry, the mountain region becomes more and more like every other part of the country. With the gains of prosperity come the loss of character, distinctiveness. Identity is increasingly a matter of money: "Phil felt that he might be in the state capital or in Washington or any other city—for these were not unique Nantahala people; they were as standardized as identical hairstyles, clothes, jokes, food, newspapers and rebellious offspring could make them. But although they were not unique, neither were they universal. Paradoxically, just as Ivy and the family were unique—exasperatingly, humorously, sadly so— they were also touched by universality and Phil knew that his mother could have walked among the people in the foreign lands he had visited and won their friendship" (314).

I know of no work of fiction that reveals more effectively the loneliness and emptiness in the lives of so many of the prosperous and powerful, the outstandingly successful, than *The Far Family* does. In the postwar boom the region has risen to undreamed-of affluence. The families with memories and roots in dirt farms are living in mansions, managing banks, mingling with factory owners, senators, and governors. Yet Phil is overwhelmed by a feeling of emptiness and pointlessness. The political world is not at all what he imagined it would be: "As he went to get the car, Phil sighed in exasperation both with himself and with the evening. He had never seen a lonelier, more desperate, group of people. They held on to their little club to show how closely they were bound together, and essentially they were as uncommitted to one another as the lion and impala of the jungle were uncommitted to each other. They made up for a lack of true community with the trappings of 'community spirit.' Words replaced actions. Symbols passed for realities" (315).

One of the special things about Dykeman's third novel, *Return the Innocent Earth* (New York: Holt, Rinehart and Winston, 1973), is that the first-person narrative sections are spoken by a contemporary male character, Jonathan Clayburn Jr. Jon is a senior vice-president of Clayburn-Durant Foods, and he is the presiding conscience and consciousness of the story. Readers and reviewers are often surprised when women authors write from a male perspective, or when male authors write from a woman's point of view. But one of the glories of fiction writing, and reading, is the discovery of the world through other eyes, other voices. The way stories connect with other lives keeps us reading, and writing, them. One of the rewards of fiction is this reaching across the boundaries of gender, geography, class, race, ethnicity, religion, even language through translation. And not least is the way fiction can give us a window on the past, stretching across generations to bring us a sense of kinship and community with those who have come before us.

Return the Innocent Earth is a dynastic story, the story of the building of a canning corporation in East Tennessee and then across the nation. It is a story of seed time and harvest, from mountain spring to the boardroom of a corporation. Most of all it is the story of a family, the Clayburn family, beginning with Elisha and Mary on their farm in the mountains, and the extended family of community and business. It is a story of growth, from pumpkin patch to preferred stock.

Return the Innocent Earth reveals an impressive knowledge of business, the methods of business and organization, the cultures of business, the ethics of business. I know of no other novel that gives such an intimate and sweeping view of the process of business growth, the setbacks and triumphs, the uncertainties and vision, decision making, and how personalities define policies as much as rules and principles. The novel should be required reading in every MBA program.

As Dykeman exhibited a considerable insight into the political world in *The Far Family*, the country club and the courthouse, she shows a special understanding of the process of manufacturing, development, research, and marketing in *Return the Innocent Earth*. She illustrates with precision and clarity the technology and experiment that go into modern business. The novel is an education in the methods of research, quality control, labor studies, environmental concerns. The novel is a portrait of industry, including both the horrors and the industrial sublime. There is a special feeling for the thrill of enterprise, competitiveness, growth, the drive toward excellence and winning.

The character Stull is the embodiment of ruthless ambition, blind ambition. Rather than cooperation, communication, team play, he relishes the fight itself, and victory, whatever the cost. His instincts are those of a killer. "Stull wanted something. And whatever it was, he wanted it exclusively and totally and at the cheapest price possible. Whoever sat opposite him was automatically an adversary. Winning was all" (8).

But Stull's cousin Jon, the narrator of much of the book and the leading character, sees competition and industry in another way. He views the company not only as its products and profits, but as the people who contribute, who do the daily work. The company includes the soil from which the crops grow, and the food to nourish and nurture a society: "This mid-town, five-story brick building grew from the wide flat cornfields surrounding this midwestern metropolis where the Durants had built a food empire, and grew from the river-bottom acres in the mountain South where the Clayburns had built their business, and grew from cool acres of clear chartreuse spring peas in Wisconsin. . . . The fragrance of ketchup gathered all up on one bouquet" (20–21).

A major theme in *Return the Innocent Earth* is the need and importance of remembering. Men like Stull have no interest in the past. They only want to move forward, toward the bigger and richer, the more powerful. But Jon Clayburn Jr. wants to keep in touch with the past, his family past, with its roots in land and place. He says, "I could remember. I needed to remember" (21). "Canning is part of two worlds and there is no escaping either. Land and computers. Seeds and machinery. Weather and sales charts. The gone-before and yet-to-come are by-products of every can we fill. Yet in those big, sleek central offices in the midwestern metropolis where I live, we lose touch" (35).

Return the Innocent Earth is Jon's act of remembering, of reconnecting. He knows that to know himself he must keep in contact with the past, with his family past, and the region's past. To lose the past is to lose the self, and lose the present and future also. We know who we are because we know what has come before us. "I come from a line of remembering people. In generations past we built churches and ballads and a way of life out of our remembering, handing down words the way others pass along designs woven into coverlets, carved in wood, or worked into clay. But now that is going, too—the woven words and the cloth and all" (36).

Clear water is a motif in *Return the Innocent Earth* just as it is in the two novels that precede it. When Jonathan Clayburn Sr. tells his dream to Cebo, he describes darkness, and narrowness, lostness, and fear. It is a dream of anxiety and confusion, until he hears the sound of water: "I heard an unbelievable sound. It was running water. When I looked I found the boldest, clearest river seen on this round globe. And I lay right down in its swift, deep current and it carried me through a passage in the mountains and out near home" (99). After he describes his dream, Cebo, the ancient voice of folklore and wisdom, responds, "That about the best luck can come, a dream of clear water."

Water is always a sign of continuity, of health, of renewal, in Dykeman's fiction. It is almost a biblical symbol of life.

Dykeman has a special understanding of the code of maleness. I can't think of a contemporary fiction writer who has portrayed better the masculine sense of self. As Jon Clayburn describes his own growth, his own recognition of what it means to become a man, to act like a man in a man's world, we recognize the accuracy of his account, the truth of his realization. "But I knew the code I had broken with Stull. Even then I knew, although I could not have put it into words. We (especially we boys, we men) were not supposed to discuss the innerness of life. We were supposed to observe true division of Sunday from Monday. We were splintered into a half-dozen fragments and our maturity was measured not by trying to make the parts into a whole but by juggling the pieces cleverly, separately, so that no one saw the empty spaces. . . . I remained acutely aware of the embarrassment most Clayburns felt in confronting or discussing the creative, spiritual, moral, sexual, intangible forces of their lives" (161–62).

Perhaps the most moving scene in the novel is that where the brother Dan has let slip an obscene phrase in front of his mother, Mary Clayburn. He and his siblings are paralyzed by the embarrassment. All wait in terror to see what the strict Mary Clayburn will do to punish him. She surprises them, and us, by ordering Dan to go out and break a hickory, then sends him back to get a larger switch, and then orders him to whip her, since if he has done wrong it is her fault. She is the mother and she is responsible. He breaks down in tears, but she will not let him off.

> The sigh of the supple bough echoed down the hall.
> "Again, Daniel. Harder."
> The sound of the striking and the crying mingled. "Much harder."
> Eventually the ordeal was finished. They heard the switch strike against the wall and fall to the floor as Dan flung it away from him. They heard him run upstairs. (188–89)

Besides her fiction and *The French Broad* Wilma Dykeman published more than a dozen books of nonfiction. With her husband, James Stokely Jr., she gave us sensitive and progressive studies of the modern South, and with her sons, Dykeman Stokely and James Stokely III, haunting portraits of the people of the Great Smokies. She enriched us with a memorable history of the battle of Kings Mountain, and the poetry of the volume called *Haunting Memories*.

IT IS AN HONOR to celebrate Wilma Dykeman, who contributed so much to the state and region with her writing. She was a grand woman of letters of a kind we don't see much anymore. She was equally at home talking with governors or rural mountain people. She served as an ambassador of history and literature to countless communities, and she was an enthusiastic champion of contemporary writers. Like a mountain spring, she gave us a bold, steady stream of sparkling words for over half a century. Her presence was an inspiration to many young writers, and she was certainly an inspiration to me. I am proud to say she is one of our region's treasures, and I am proud that she belongs to us here, in the mountains. Her work will continue to refresh, inform, delight, and inspire us for years and generations to come.

—Robert Morgan

PREFACE

WILMA DYKEMAN WAS BORN in 1920 in an Arts and Crafts / Adirondack-style bungalow near the head of Beaverdam Creek just north of Asheville, North Carolina. Her father was a sixty-year-old retired dairy farmer from upstate New York, her mother a twenty-three-year-old descendant of western North Carolina pioneers and preachers. Wilma grew up as an only child surrounded by mountains: Elk Mountain to the north, Iron Ore Ridge to the south, Rice Knob and Craven Gap on the future Blue Ridge Parkway to the east. For companionship, she depended mostly on plants, animals, water, and other natural features. At the age of thirty-five, she would write the first full-fledged economic argument against water pollution ever published.

The path from a girl raised in nature to a groundbreaking environmentalist (*The French Broad*, 1955), civil rights advocate (*Neither Black nor White*, 1957), and novelist (*The Tall Woman*, 1962) was not a straightforward one. Wilma's early dramatic endeavors in childhood poems and plays spoke to her desire to become an actress. Her dreams nearly came true in 1938 when the famed drama teacher Alvina Krause told Wilma, then a junior at Northwestern University, that she would become a star. By the spring of 1940, Wilma had lined up a job teaching broadcasting at Finch Junior College in Manhattan. But something interrupted her plan to move to the big city: she met the love of her life that August, back at the Beaverdam bungalow. She and James R. Stokely Jr. were married on October 12, 1940.

The newlyweds built a stone cottage in the English Mountains of Cocke County just across the state line in Tennessee. There they tried their hand at writing, James concentrating on poetry, Wilma on short stories and a novel about the Beaverdam Valley. Wilma's ambition and energy also compelled her to expand into other activities, as chronicled in her frequent letters to her mother:

> 3/2/1942: I plug at my book a little. It goes so slowly. I sometimes doubt if I have anything to say anyway, and why I don't just throw the whole thing over. But I go on.
>
> 5/9/1942: I am trying to work on a radio play series adapted from Wolfe, pertaining to the war. About 6 under the big heading: "The Promise of America!" I hope they'll be good—good enough to rouse a production somewhere. . . .
>
> Well, I'll soon be 22, and by heaven and all the stars in it, I mean to do something this year that will make it a memorable year—that is, if I shall do anything. I'm going to write myself empty, and I'm going to write something good—or throw down the effort forever! I believe I can do it.

The Beaverdam novel (entitled *The Valley*) received a bad reception in New York in the spring of 1943. In August, Gilbert Govan, the book review editor for the *Chattanooga Times*, sent Wilma her first book for review, Robert Penn Warren's *At Heaven's Gate*. "So if I can't write 'em," wrote Wilma to her mother, "maybe I can review 'em." Then, two months later, came a new venture:

> 10/21/1943: The weather has been wonderful, warm in the sun, cool shade, and all the leaves falling. . . . Have worked a little on my *new* book—there are only half-a-dozen epics under way now.

The new book was *Family of Earth*. Wilma had decided to give nonfiction a try, and what better to describe than the people, places, and emotions of her formative self? Surely she hoped that writing about what she knew most deeply would resonate with others. Perhaps more important, the memoir would enshrine her parents in words on paper, and would capture her own early selves.

Family of Earth, a memoir from an unknown Southern mountain female twentysomething, never had a chance with New York publishers. The manuscript was put away, and with the accretion of years and other priorities, was lost for the remainder of the author's life. Perhaps its publication now will help bring Wilma Dykeman the broader recognition she always deserved.

—Jim Stokely

EDITOR'S NOTE

THE ORIGINAL MANUSCRIPT of *Family of Earth* is
typewritten with frequent handwritten edits by the author
and her husband. She added in two instances a handwritten
paragraph or two, and once a full handwritten section about
snow at the end of Chapter 5.

My guiding principle throughout has been to leave the
original as intact as possible. I have made minor changes
silently to enhance clarity or to correct grammatical errors.

—Jim Stokely

....

FAMILY OF EARTH

....

THERE WERE ALWAYS THOSE among us who loved life and knew it, who were never satiated by any of its simple duties or routine demands. But most of us forgot what life was until now, when war and death have come close to us and, in the tradition of Mephistopheles, asked us to sign away that trifle, life.

We awaken, we look about us—we listen to the musical thrush of life all around, we breathe, we taste, and suddenly we know that life was always within us, here inside and encompassing our every step. Suddenly, too, our loneliness has been thrust into our consciousness, and we realize that in this final imperative challenge we are each alone to answer as we will and can. What my mother and father would do, I know. But what we will do is something more complex. Do we find enough of the still woods, the remote stars, the long solitudes, within our souls to accept this loneliness and grow toward death as inevitably as the water before my house runs to the lake where it will merge into a whole and at last be still?

Perhaps some will believe that this book is of no contemporary moment, that it does not deal directly with "the situation" which is at hand. But the earth is with us always and we are one family upon it. It is peace upon this earth for which we fight—good peace; it is life upon this earth for which we die—full life. It is what our peace and life have meant to us in yesterday that will enable us to fight and die today.

Perhaps, too, I can hope that this book will mean more than yesterday or today, something also of tomorrow. And if to any it appears presumptuous to write a book about one's life, especially when that life has been so unimportant, then all I can answer is this: first, it is the only life I know intimately enough to write about and say what I would say; and second, every life, no matter how inconsequential in the tide of nationalities, has overtones of the universal and themes which are common to all men and all nature.

For each of us, there is a time that comes in our lives when we can look at the past and at the future and see them briefly, in sharp outline against the momentary pattern. This time is swift, and sudden and unexpected. It simply says, softly and unmistakably, "Now you are no longer a boy or a girl; you are grown. A man or woman." Then the second has gone, and the realization remembered has only whispered itself to you.

The world has changed. Or, perhaps more truly stated, you have changed toward the world. The perspective has shifted. The uncertain, unsteady birth pangs of a new phase of living grasp the mind, and everything learned must be relearned, everything stated must be restated.

This moment came for me after my father's death. There was a funeral, which I disremember. Then my mother left for New York with his body, for that was where he was buried. We stood in the railway station and waited for the train to leave. I could see mother's face in the square little opening of glass. She looked so unlike what she had ever been before that I could almost feel I did not know her. Her face was white with a pallid unhealthy whiteness that made her brown eyes appear over-large and strangely wounded, like the hurt eyes of some small stabbed animal which cannot understand its persecutor. It twisted my heart to see her face there in the window looking so.

With a great puff of steam and a screaming lurch of cars and brakes and engine, the train began to move. With a sickening sorrow, regret engulfed me; engulfed me for the words unsaid, the things undone, the moments only half completed. If time and the train could have stood for only a breath, only a space just wide enough to catch some of the raveled edges, some of the dangling threads. But the train did not stop. It gathered speed. Now the window was gone from sight, and already the engine was rounding the curve ahead. Like a rolling earthworm, the cars followed behind, roaring down the tracks, heading toward other places and other people. Around the curve they went and disappeared from sight.

The air was noticeably silent after the roll of sound. Even the paper boy was peddling his news without the shouted jargon of a minute ago. People hurried out of the station, bound for home and business. The rain dripped off the shed-like roof of the outer platform, and was quite visible, now that the train had gone. With steady precision the drops gathered, then fell with little puddling splashes.

I was quite alone. There were people there, some of my family, some of our friends. But I was alone—with the rain and the silent station and the quick preoccupied strangers. I knew that life would never be the same again, and vaguely I sensed that I would never be the same. (Oh, the mind is capable of quite dramatic realizations during these intensified moments of existence.) One of the props which I had depended on was gone, and from now on I would stand at least half-alone. There was responsibility too, and I had already begun to taste of that; and there would be thought of money, and the place, and all the new-found burdens which my mother would assume.

It was true. From that day on, I sensed responsibilities never explicitly given me. I learned of practicality. I learned something of the variability of people. With my father's death, there came a shift in many attitudes of friends, of even family. I would scarcely have guessed that such a shift were possible. In short, I exchanged many young illusions for disillusion, and perhaps gained new, more bitter, deceptions in the bargain. I found less time for dreaming over a crawfish in the pond, less time for hunting where a lady slipper grew.

So it was we left our childhood and the peace that was a part of it. Now we had grown into a problematical world where answers were few and the truth was seldom unalloyed. We were our own questioners and the only source of answers to those questions. We looked and saw the rain along the dingy roof tops, saw the rain falling in the soot-filled apron of the city, and could hear the whistle far away of the train which bore our father and our mother.

THE TRUTH of the planets rolling through space with that mathematical precision which seems at once so accidental and so planned, is to me no more glorious or awful than the truth of two human beings born in different times and distant places, following through their life a pattern at once so accidental and so planned that in its course of unbelievable days and events they shall meet somewhere, somehow, and know one another. The mystery of how many thousands of years in the past, the tales of how many millions of people gone, will enter into the retelling of a tale as old and unique as life itself?

So it came about, by accident or plan, that in the eighteenth century while a Dutch settler was founding his home and raising his family in the then outskirts of a city called New Amsterdam, a Scotch-Irish wanderer in the Southern Appalachians had begun a family whose rambles were to carry them over the entire region of mountains where they were to build their homes. The Dutch family grew strong and worthy. They contributed a captain to the Revolution; they entered into the politics of a state which was to become a leader of the Union. They did not hurry to the wealth which was then so easy for the opportunist, but lived near the land, knowing the roots of their strength. Down in the mountains, the Scotch-Irish settled themselves and sang their ballads, built what they needed and grew what they ate, felt the seasons and humors of nature and waxed philosophical and humorous.

12-20-2016 4:53PM
Item(s) checked out to Carroll, Deborah

TITLE: An Alzheimer's guide : activities
BARCODE: 31815012613406
DUE DATE: 01-10-17

And in 1859, when there were yet only thirty-three states in the Union, when the land from Iowa to Oregon, from Missouri to California, was only a vast unsettled territory, and when men sat around their fireplaces and discussed the coming election of 1860, which was to be one of the most momentous in all history—between a lawyer named Lincoln and an orator named Douglas—a boy was born in a frame farmhouse in New York's Putnam County. He was named Willard Jerome Dykeman. Two years after his birth, his state was at war with the section which would someday be his home.

Thirty-seven years later, in 1896, when men were discussing an election which was one of the most spectacular in all our history—between McKinley from Ohio and Bryan from Nebraska—a girl was born in the mountains of North Carolina. She was named Bonnie Ballard Cole. Two years after her birth, her uncles who were of age left for service in the Spanish-American War.

But before the girl was ever born, Willard Dykeman had gone to North Carolina. In the wander-hunger of youth he had spent a lonely year herding sheep with a mountain for his range and a small town named Asheville for his guide. What things did a young man far from home, isolated with the wind and mountains and sheep, think on? What did he find, being nineteen and with a country wide before him, to make him return home and build a life and family there? For return he did. In New York, he married and farmed and raised two children. Then that cycle of his life ended. His wife was dead, his farm work well done and no desire for more money, his children grown. And so again, he came to the mountains. Again he rested near Asheville—this time in the valley lying at the foot of the mountain where he had stayed when he was nineteen and the world was open before him.

This was when the long-begun cycle completed itself—when the Dutch and the Scotch-Irish, the North and the South, the mountains and the fertile farmlands—fateful opposite that each

....

was, met and knew one another. For strange and peculiar pole-star it was that led Willard Dykeman and Bonnie Cole to meet in this time and bring to their union the religion of nature and the philosophy of loneliness.

THE HOUSE my father and mother built soon after they were married, in which I was born, and where we lived until I was six years old, was a log house sitting back from the road among thick pines. The creek for which the valley was named, Beaverdam, ran in front of it. It was a comfortable picturesque house, with a long porch running along the front and the length of one whole side. In front of the side entrance stood three dogwoods, beautiful in the spring, and at the front entrance stood pines, beautiful in the winter. The steps to the house were great wide stones, showing the mark of my father's drill, where he had been forced to cut them away from the parent boulder. Directly behind the house, and built into the side of a bank, was a cellar. There was a heavy door to the cellar and a carved latch which my father had made himself. Standing in the cellar, there was the damp cool feel of earth and the odor of broken roots mingling with the odors of apples and vegetables and cured meat. To me, this was a dark mysterious place, as cavernous and inestimable as all the belly hunger of man.

The house itself had a large living room, with a fireplace in one side; a kitchen with windows facing east and west; two bedrooms, each with a fireplace; a dining room; and a room we called the music room. In here stood a tremendous rose-wood piano, dark and shiny, with a red plush-covered bench to sit upon. Sometimes I would go alone into the room and raise the long piano lid. There were the keys in their neat invariable arrangement of black and white. If only I knew the language, I could make the darkness of the piano speak to me. But the world outside was sweet and warm and there were many languages to learn.

This was a fine world for a child to know. It touched the imagination; in fact, it required the imagination. For without the spark of story-telling and fancy, it would have been a lonesome world. But there was a broad field on one side, where red clover grew in summer and bees pursued their busy noisy life with many comings and goings. On the other side and behind were woods, and many little rises and falls and curious shapings of the earth. In front was the moving water.

Each portion of the place was a continent entire, with its scurrying lives and growing plants. Each moment lived in any part was a reflection of all time, and made the measurements of clock and calendar seem strangely without meaning.

THE VALLEY proper stretched from the little promontory where the Baptist country church stood, to the ring of mountains which formed the head of the valley. Branching from the main highway were many tributary roads which ran up the small canyons and coves formed in turn by parts of the mountains which stretched out from the main long line of peaks like fingers reaching from an ageless hand. Up these coves the people had settled, making for themselves a place in the friendly, yet foreboding, presence of the hills.

Strangers in the valley usually noticed the white frame church. We who lived there naturally never did. Its presence on the horizon was as passive as the usual participation in the activities behind the stained oak doors. But on going around the curve, and looking up from the valley, there was often such beauty that even we could not resist but must sometimes pause and wonder at it. Beyond the hillside graves and stones of the country cemetery, the valley opened, and like a cup, sloped from a narrow base up to a wide round openness. Surrounding were the mountains, which reached from their sprawling base to a wide and distant sky. Sometimes along the sides were faint dents where some one or two, not content with the coves, had cut and built; but these patches were near the valley floor, and the rim of the hills was left untouched.

Driving up the concrete road, we passed such farms and houses as had become landmarks through the years. We would say, "Down by the road where the old Fitchett house stands," or "Across from Bob Stradley's spring house under the maples." In between the older landmarks were the smaller houses, cabins, cottages, such as one finds in any land or time.

There was an end to the concrete, and a forking of the road. The fork to the right led up past an apple orchard, around the side of the mountain, until at last it joined with a scenic highway which many people from the town drove in the summer afternoons. The fork on the left followed a mountain creek by a dairy, led past a white square house on a hill, past a log house sitting in the pines, and went at last on by another white square house and ended as a road, beyond several mountain cabins built at good distances between each other. From these cabins on, the road was merely a tree-covered trail, good for horses, or a sled, but little else. We lived on the road to the left.

But with the ending of the concrete highway, and the beginning of crushed stone, or gravel, there was a significant dividing line in other things than stone. From the black-draped woman's figure we often saw crossing the road at the first grey house on the left of our fork, past the silos, to the mountain cabins further up where the road became steep and narrow, all were different from the houses, and the sense of houses, where the pavement ran. And the poorest of them all, the cabin shacks, the rough frame houses, were nearest to that stretch of blue and grey above the mouthpiece of the cuplike hills.

This was the way of the valley when I was a child. It was a memorable thing in winter to drive along the road and see the early fog settling down over the coves at five o'clock of an afternoon. Slowly, silently, with the drifting measuredness of time, it surrounded the trees, flowed down the hills, and shifted from sight the contours of the land. We could watch it moving toward the hill behind our house, and knew that when we reached home we would be in the midst of a cloud, a wet moving greyness that would make the edges of the world seem limitless, and ourselves set far apart in an uninhabited solitude.

Or it was memorable of a summer evening to watch the blending of colors scattered by the sun. Rich as a fabulous carpet is rich, the shadows lay soft and deep over the hillsides, rising and falling in a blend of purple and blue and green. There was a sense of luxury and mellowness in the mountains then.

The people, too, were intricate and varied, with all the intricacy and variety so unsuspected and so characteristic of simple people. They worked and played and hunted, bore children, died and dug in patches of rocky ground. Each was memorable in his own separate way.

Between the background and the people, our lives lay more with the mountains than the people, for we knew them with more kinship and more intimacy. We could adapt ourselves to the moods of nature, find beauty in the wilder, crueler moments, reconcile the terror and the loveliness, the bird song and the preying claw; but the cruelties and kindnesses, the largeness and the pettiness were more difficult to reconcile in humans. And all were present in the valley.

IN THE EARLIEST days of spring, often before the winter ice has completely melted away and while the water still stands cold and green, frog eggs are to be found in the ponds and leaf-filled pools. They float in the water and fill the pond with their gelatinous dotted substance. There is something complete and elemental about those masses of eggs.

In the days when time was something limitless and gentle, I used to sit for hours beside our pond, studying with all the solemn imaginative gravity of a child's mind, on those frog embryos. At first, they are nothing more than round black specks in the midst of a colorless jelly. Gradually, the speck grows larger, the nourishment of that colorless jelly grows less and less. Then one day, the black dot has become a live thing—a tadpole swimming in the water. A tadpole, large of tail, hiding under the leaves and scum, suddenly alive in the midst of a world which must seem immeasurable and boundless.

Often I hauled these eggs and tadpoles out of the pond, put them on a rock and tried to create in my mind the complete cycle of becoming alive. I could see the stages of life before me but I could not spell the intermediate mysteries. Oh, how good were those mornings—cold with the last fury of winter, fresh with the first hint of spring, when the birds sang early and the water stood cold and green in the pond suddenly alive with a vast mystery of the first eggs of life.

The life of one human is the life of every other living thing on earth which must eat and seek the sun and reproduce. It is the life of every other human. Yet, at the same time, it is something unique to him, something different from any other life that has ever been. All life is kin and all men are brothers, yet each is a stranger, one to the other, and will always be so.

one

....

THAT FIRST YEAR OF LIFE—how remote it is in the annals of memory. As remote as our thousands of ancestors who dwelt in caves and roamed a terrifying world. How helpless those first men must have felt when they realized that they faced lands given over entirely to the plant kingdom and the beasts which filled the seas and swamps and plains.

We wonder if a baby's birth does not hark back to those primeval peoples and times. He is born as other animals are born, without benefit of clothes or possessions outside his own body, and how solitary is his appearance in the world. All the keynotes intimating what will come in later times are present in that overture. The dominant theme is loneliness.

So each of us comes into the world in the same manner. And the first sound we utter is a cry. We lie on our back and beat the air with our fists and find no recognition for the people about us. We have reverted to the primitive—or maybe we are just emerging from the primitive—and this is a time of eating, sleeping, and simply lying and looking around us. This is the way of all newborn things, a dog, a kitten, or a baby; and how sharply I have always sympathized with a newborn calf. Somehow, it is the very epitome of the unsteadiness and lack of self-confidence in everything young.

But what takes place in that first year? When does the fresh papyrus of memory begin to record the cuneiform symbols of what was said, or who dropped the white china plate and broke it to bits, or when the sun shone or the snow fell? I only know that I can remember my father pushing a wooden baby carriage around the porch of our brown log house. I lay in the carriage, warm under blankets, and the air was cold on my face. Tears of coldness filled my father's eyes, deep-set grey eyes they were, and a single drop of water formed on the end of his nose. He sang a song about a poor little chick-a-dee-dee. The time rose and fell in a melody of pathos and quietness.

Music was one of the first stimuli to draw a response from me. That was as it should be. What else can speak so freely and so directly to the emotions? Daddy and Mother owned a new Victrola with the little picture of the dog listening to "his master's voice." They had records of Caruso, Schumann-Heink, and Alma Gluck. Today, whenever I hear some of the songs we had on those old records, I feel a sadness stir deep inside me, as if a long dormant muscle had suddenly twinged with consciousness. It is a part of the old everlasting and familiar sadness which we experience when we listen to some profound passage of music and feel the revelation of a memory so long past we cannot recall its shapes or name its presence, but only know that it exists. Music is the perfect combination between our fundamental biologic lives and the fibres of our souls.

For a whole year I lived in a world foreign to me. I had no way of communication, the sounds of language were so much gibberish in my ears. I did not understand what I saw, and everyone was alien. It was an insatiable curiosity that kept me fascinated. I felt heat and cold, dampness and softness, and the handling of many hands. From the darkness and warmth of my mother's womb I had been plunged into a world where eyes and ears and hands were all needed in a struggle for existence and comprehension.

Then I began to crawl. How did I sense the feel of scuttling over the floor on my hands and knees? Where did I learn such a feat? In some dusky dim past, or was it simply the easiest solution to a problem of balance?

Then at the end of the strangest year of life, when I had already learned the only essential lesson—the lesson of loneliness—I was crawling, and feeling with my hands the roughness of floors, the softness of rugs, and the warmth of the earth.

One

two

....

AT TWO I BEGAN to establish contact with the world. No longer was I the wide-eyed spectator of the panorama which went forward around me every day. No longer did I lie in my small white bed or sit on the floor with a round red ball and listen with troubled ignorance to what those people near me said. The greatest step of my acclimatizing process was over, although the process itself had only just begun, and would be endless. I was ready to begin participating in this series of events and days which I certainly did not understand, and of which I could only dimly realize the haziest outlines. If I had but known then that this participation in the drama, once begun, could never be revoked except by death, that it was always irrevocably moving forward and could never be stopped or sidetracked for a minute—if I had realized this, I say, perhaps I would have observed longer from my vantage point of babyhood and isolation. Probably I would have done just what I did do—plunged into the current as soon as I found out how to perform some of the tricks.

Walking was the first of those tricks. What an event it was to stand on one's own feet, unsteady as they might be, and look about him. Who can appreciate the sense of power that merely standing may impart to a person? Surely only someone who has never stood before can taste its sweetest virtues. There is a sweet self-confidence in being able to balance one's own body, hold it erect by the strength of his bones, feel the weight and the rhythm of its pressure on his feet. It is a moment to look at the dubious uncles and aunts, the fearful grandmother, the expectant and hopeful parents, and say, with the language of your body, "I can stand alone."

It is to relish the triumph of that victory and then it is to put one hesitant foot forward and balance the head and arms and trunk and to speak once again with your body, "More, I can walk."

So the clutching fingers, the protecting arms, are put away. Now there is no need for the guiding and tutoring hands. The first lesson is well learned. And now, with this first liberation, I have given up, too, the sweetness of being carried. I have assumed the proportions of an individual, I have become aware of myself. Through the groping unaccustomed workings of my mind, with the aid of environment and instinct and patterns before me, I have come to a realization of the power that lies within me. It is a latent unharnessed strength, but I gather it to myself, I take hold of its possibilities, and lo, an act of locomotion has been miraculously accomplished. I have moved all that I possess half-way across this room, and my legs have carried me well. I am a moving object upon the earth, my roots are of the spirit—I shall walk far.

Again, what other mobile creature upon the face of the land can stand erect, but man? Has not his backbone, the miraculous thread called a spinal column, set him apart from all his fellow animals? That, plus the uses he has made of his brain, the development he has undergone, through centuries of time, which increased and specialized the functions of that brain. But physically, pictorially, he is the sole mammal which walks erect, has appendages which he calls hands, and can by the nature of his posture hold his head more aptly toward the sky.

This is no small matter then, our first step alone in this aging world which has witnessed so many quivering steps. But the infinite numbers which have been in the past, or which are to come in the future, cannot diminish the splendor of this single

Tuo

....

15

step of mine. For it alone, with or without the other millions of steps, is an assertion of species, which is the right of every living thing—and a mute triumph of lone splendor, which is the birthright of man as long as he lives on this planet.

In my second year another tremendous event occurred. I learned to talk. I had reasoned out the symbols and the sounds and what they represented in reality. Now I could enter into magic communication with other people.

When I first spoke, it was not to repeat any word or murmur someone's name. It was an entire sentence, three connected words. My mother was carrying me along the road to my grandmother's, and she walked by the brook before our house. Suddenly, I pointed toward the gleaming moving water. "Waddy coming down," I said. How fortunate I was to have some object for attention so suggestive and so natural as this mountain creek to make me speak. Of what can children in cities speak, when they see no stretches of woods or ribbons of water?

There it had been before me, the clear deep water, pouring over the jagged stones, making a sweet natural music, and I had felt rise in me words which would tell what I saw. The elements of nature and the spirits of children are close kin.

So I began to carry on conversation, limited at first to wants and needs, but broadened gradually as there was more to say and growing understanding for what was said. Words held a charm for me. Later I would become lost in the beauty of a single word, pondering on all it might suggest, what pictures it might conjure in my mind, or in someone else's mind, and all the ways it might be used. They were common words—an adjective like purity, a noun like glass, or a verb like hop—but I could handle them and coat them over with magic and make them into symbols of unbelievable stature.

My father and mother read aloud a great deal. Before an open wood fire in our fireplace we would sit, my mother reading from some book or magazine, and her soft voice moved out over the room and filled it with people and places. When I was very small, before I knew many words, I would hear her speak one now and again which caught my fancy. Then I would break the spell of the book, finding out what the word meant and asking them to use it in sentences for me. One of those words was boomerang. Queer word that it should fix itself in my mind, or that I should remember learning it, after all these years.

Now, indeed, I had begun life. By one act, I had established my independence and solitary nature; by the other I had woven an indivisible thread of contact and sociability between myself and other people.

Little wonder when they tell us that during the first three years of a person's life he learns more than he will ever learn all the rest of his years put together.

three

....

ALL THE MEMORIES of my first six years, and later, are bound up and intertwined with the odor of wood, the feel of shavings curled through the finger, the sound of rip-saw or hammer. For my father's workshop was rich in the sensory appeals and the peaceful atmosphere which a child can never forget.

It was an atmosphere filled with the raw fine odor of wood newly sawed, freshly sandpapered. The sawdust lay in little golden and brown heaps over the floor. It gave a fine sensation running through cupped hands—like watching the orange sand slip through an hourglass someone gave me later.

Here in his workshop, making things for a hobby, my father was an artist. Outside he might be ordinary, but in this realm he was an artist. When he ran his hand along the length of a board, the very wood seemed to become alive under his fingers, seemed to follow the feel of his touch and begin to shape itself into the new form it was to take under his guidance. When he took a tool in his hand, and held it for a moment as if weighing all the possibilities and angles of its use, that tool—whether it was his smallest auger or his machine-run saw—seemed to blend into his hand and follow his designs easily, naturally. For he had a respect for all that he used, and especially for the woods. Never did it seem that he twisted or forced a piece to his own desires, into a shape it did not want. Rather, it was as if he simply took one living form and shaped it into another form.

Black walnut was his favorite wood. Cherry, oak, he sometimes used, but always he returned to walnut. "There's something strong and good about it," he said.

Once years later my half brother [Jerome Dykeman] sent a piece of mahogany from South America to be made into a table. It was a red and golden wood, beautiful like silky hair with variations of light thrown on it. I had just read Hudson's *Green Mansions* at the time, and with the coming of this length of alien lumber, my imagination loosed its bars and tried to picture where this beauty of a tree had fallen, in what jungles and by what waters it had grown, and—greatest of all—had a Rima perhaps leaped from its branches?

The table my father made was a graceful thing—dainty, with curving thin legs and finely polished surface. Somehow, though, once inside the house, it looked out of place. It stood like an elegant jungle bird might have stood among our plain catbirds and brown thrashers. When it was finished, my father returned to the walnut, building a Mission-style piece or two, making the rare golden lights in the dark walnut glow with a lustre which only sure hands could have drawn to the surface.

So it was that he made furniture for our house. Seeing the need for a certain piece, or wanting to make a special object, he would begin in his workshop the service of love. Slowly, slowly, he would turn the square piece in his lathe; gently, he would fit two matching notches, one into the other, until they became one whole; firmly, he would plane the surfaces and smooth the roughness. Slowly, gently, firmly, until a strong simple part of our home stood there before him and he found it to his satisfaction. It is few today who have a sense for fine woods, for textures.

I can see my father now in his workshop. One long room with a table running the length of the room, and above the table, tools hanging in graduated sizes each after each in long rows. Hammers, saws, files, squares, planes—these and so many other tools, that a child's eyes and fancy ran away with her, and

I could not imagine what uses my father found for all the implements he owned. Often he would say to me, as I stood watching with bird-bright eyes, "It's not so much what you have as the way you use it; the way you keep it." Then he might speak of a common Southern fault, his chin firm with earnestness, "Now you take people around here. They leave their tools and farm things out in the weather, free to all the rain and sun and snow. Then they wonder why they don't have anything. If they'd only take care of what they do have."

I have seen him grow angry and sorry on different occasions about just such carelessness. Just as he so often grew angry or sorry at the same time over all the lost efforts and wasted talents of men's lives, and his own impotence to bring about a change in them.

And oh, it was very good to stand in the strong masculinity of his workroom and feel the living quality of the wood as it shaped under his knotty, homely hands—to stand and watch him reach for tool or nail with steady certainty that he would find it in its rightful place because he had seen to it that it should be there. The fact of his reaching restored assuredness and made even a child, who had found in childish things that life is not always sure, feel that there *was* plan, and that somewhere, somehow, there was order.

My grandmother had a touch for cloth. She could feel a bolt with her finger and the quality seemed to speak to her. It was so with all the older women who had learned to make their clothes and counted the cost of woolens and cottons and silks. Today the quality has gone, replaced by quantity. A mass of manufactured skimpy "frocks," instead of a few wide-seamed, fine material dresses.

It was not so with my father and his furniture. He chose the texture of wood, and the grain; veneer was ugly and camouflage to him. Square strength and simplicity marked his workmanship. There were no furbelows, as is often so, to hide errors in wood or work.

I SPENT much time when I was small with my grandmother. Her name was Loretta Ballard Cole. She was a small, brown-eyed woman with wavy white hair and an intelligent face. During her whole life, she had never been free from financial worries. She was the oldest child of a Baptist preacher, and when her mother had died when she was seventeen, she had helped raise a family of seven. It had been no small task. Then she herself had married a witty handsome man who was able to give her much, but never security. They had seven children, too, the second of which was my mother. At forty-three, grandpa died, and grandma was left with little but her own skill and ingenuity. Yet there was no miserliness or broodiness about her, as has come to many women faced with such problems. I suppose it was because she was inherently a philosopher, a person who accepted much and had found an inner life. For her, this inner life had been religion, which she had followed with much faith and in which she had found much strength.

I was her first grandchild, born a month after her husband died, and she petted me. "Your head's like a little peeled onion it's so bare," she said, "and your hands are like little bird-claws. But I think you're the sweetest little onion-bird I ever saw."

Sometimes she would tell me about her early teaching, before she was married, how she rode side-saddle over the hills to teach in the rough one-room building where the first grade through the eighth grade was the extent of studies and all grades sat together.

"I was slim then," she would say. "Oh yes, as slim as your mother. And I had a black riding suit I wore; oh, you should have seen me. Of course, some of the boys were larger than I was, and when I first went there I suppose they thought that—well, me being so slight and all, they could just do as they pleased. But they found out to the contrary. Yes, they did. I was there to teach them, and I did. I taught them to read and spell and work arithmetic, and if they never learned another thing, I know they knew those three. And I'll tell you something, I'm pretty good

Three

....

at spelling myself. Even if I did learn it at a wee little mountain school."

She was often using words like "wee," words which others around did not use, which had a poetical sound to them. I liked to hear her talk for this reason: because you never knew just how she was going to say a thing.

She was a good speller, that was so. I have heard her spell words since that no one else in the room could spell, and *that* when she was trained with the blue-backed speller and learning came second, and far second, to the necessities of living. I never heard her make a grammatical error, either, and she has often corrected many of us who have studied more recently from the "advanced" grammar books. Grammatical errors are common to mountain folks; ignorance is happiness to many of them. Yet, somehow, there was planted a strain in her that made her rise above surroundings and find what was correct in the use of words, made her look beyond ignorance to the pastures of learning and urged her forward to those very pastures.

One of grandma's greatest interests was making quilts. I would watch her when I was small, wondering at the speed with which she could manipulate a needle. In and out, in and out, through the bright colored squares and triangles and circles. All the pieces seemed very small at first, as if they would require (in my impatient mind) an eternity to grow into a quilt. Grandma would have a cotton bag filled with scraps and waste pieces of material. These she would cut into her little shapes and sew them, one by one, together. Then suddenly, the more she sewed, a pattern began to emerge. The Wedding Ring, the Chinese Plate, the Star. Any of these she might make, and others. I would look at all the squares, and she would ask me what color I would use to set them together with. Then we would ponder and deliberate on the different shades in the different squares. She was very particular about her colors, and wanted them to blend and have a pleasant harmony. I would name a color, and then she would agree or disagree. I would watch her set the pieces together later, and I would see where her reasons had been right. In most of these quilts I could find some of the materials which were familiar to me. I had known them either in a dress of mother's or one of my own, or in one of grandma's dresses. It was somehow startling and pleasant to have a material long forgotten suddenly appear again, fresh and bright, in the design of a beautiful quilt. And grandma's quilts were beautiful. They blended into a pattern, and were made of material good and strong, as well as colorful and pretty. And when they were completed, they were something more than the sum of their parts. Between the thousands of small even stitches which marched across and around the pattern, there was a blending of skill and patience and personality made tangible. I have never since seen a handmade quilt hanging in a craft-shop window, or displayed in some department store, but I have thought of the woman who made it, and of grandma, and found a warm glow at the beauty of their artistry which can take a common needle and a jumble of colors and create something as necessary, if perhaps not so great, as any painter's picture or any writer's song.

four

WHEN I WAS FOUR we went on our first camping trip. There were to be many others during the course of the years, to various sections, with various people, but none which could remain in my memory with the same half-real, half-imagined fancy of that first trip, together.

It was in the late spring, hovering on early summer, and we went with our beautiful horse, Trixie, leading the way before our queer little buggy. Spring in the air is indescribable, though so many people have tried to pin it down on paper, but the day must have been a memorable thing of sunshine and blue sky and happiness to my father and mother. To me, being four, it was the creature comforts of a warm little coat, a feeling of security between the two people on each side of me in the seat of the buggy, and an occasional drink of cold water to taste sweet and pure inside my thirsty mouth. Perhaps I remember vaguely the tallness of the mountains we drove through, or the fine views we were able to see from a certain road; but I remember clearly the jolt of the wheels as we rode along and the steady rhythm of Trixie's movements.

The one thing I do remember with no faltering, or no spurring of the memory, is the morning. It was the morning after we had camped by the river. There has never been another morning, before or since, that was like it. What happened the night before, or what came in the time following, I do not know.

All I know is that there was an hour before sunrise which was beautiful. It clipped itself out of the surrounding hours like a newspaper clipping set aside from all the rest of a bulky paper, and kept to be referred to again and again in the coming time. It might even have been called a moment of sanctuary.

We had camped some distance from a large old farmhouse, in a meadow. The meadow might once have been used for a pasture, but now it bordered on a patch of woods and had grown up in tall grasses and weeds. At the foot of the meadow was a great creek, almost large enough to be called a river, it rushed along so hard and fast. Across the creek, quite some distance away, was a barn. It was the first thing we made out when we woke up in the morning. Its bulky dark shadow loomed through the mist and gave no hint of what it might be, but we guessed at it, and our guesses proved correct.

Remembering a thing like that morning, the memory is not spread out, as in a continuous series of events or occurrences, but is steady and whole as in a picture. A picture glimpsed, felt, drunk in, in that moment when its vision was revealed. And so the conglomerate impressions at once were intertwined with each other. That is the way they remain in my mind.

There was the feeling. Who has ever been on a camping trip and not felt that swift stabbing chill of early morning air as it hits him in the face and goes through his clothes as if they were nothing, to wrap the body in goose-pimply flesh? There was dampness rising in the mist from the river-creek, which made the hands moist and clammy, made one feel as if he were in some unknown climate. There was the feel of this dampness on the face, erasing any drowsiness which might remain from the night with the warm, heavy blankets.

There were the odors. Subtle odors of morning; water smell from the creek, wet earth and crushed grass where we had walked, the almost sterile quality of the air as if it had been washed clean of intruding odors during the night before. Then the smoke. Wood smoke in the early morning air! Such a human fragrance, overcoming more delicate smells with its own strong pungency. And combining with it, the odors of coffee and eggs and bacon, even more human, stirring some primitive urge in the pit of the stomach, until it would almost seem as if we were set back a thousand years or so and had emerged in this mist with only the cravings of our hunger and thirst and love.

Mother set me in the buggy, out of the dew to keep my feet dry, while she and my father fixed the fire and breakfast, and I could look about me and see the wet fresh world. It looked like a newborn chicken, damp, not quite alert to the urgency of sun. The fog had been heavy during the night and, combined with the mist from the river, had drenched the trees, the grass, everything about us with a dewy moisture which was unlike rain in that its quality was ephemeral, would pass quickly with the actuality of day. Even now, the pale yellow rays were spraying through the fog, bringing a glimmer of warmth and color into the grayness. The barn in the distance was edgeless, without shape. Its height and breadth were indeterminate, fading into the mist. It might have been a prehistoric cave, or shapeless dragon of fear, looming in the unknown beyond the creek and just outside our little world.

The quietness and sense of space was shattered by the familiar sound of a horse's whinny. Trixie raised her head, her ears alert, pointed for the sound to come again. It came, and she replied. The animals on the farm had sensed the presence of another horse, perhaps had known it by some deep-rooted instinct, and had established contact with the stranger. Through the rising of the fog and the drying off of the moisture on the ground and branches, they whinnied to each other again, then again. There were other sounds too. The crowing of a rooster, still farther off than the horses, coming steadily and with a mystery lent by the distance.

So I sat in the buggy and heard the sounds, smelled the odors which the morning had brought forth, and was aware of some quality which was beyond any of the five imperfect senses, which included them all and yet was greater than the sum of their impressions. It was a mystery, an other-worldness, that sometimes visits people when they catch a glimpse of some unfamiliar portion of the universe. There was a sense of the early beginnings of man, of the dawn of the world, of the swift-moving strangeness of time, and of the age when man lived on the nourishment of nature before the cutting of the umbilical cord. This, I say, is a part of what I sensed in the morning.

Then the eggs were ready, their big golden eyes warm and tasty in the hungry mouth, and we sat around our buggy and ate with marvelous appetites. The farmer brought his horses down to water at the creek. A curl of smoke was coming from his chimney now. Guineas were crying in the distance. We ate and watched the sun rise around us. The mist was gone and the day had really begun.

WHO CAN REMEMBER the people of his childhood and write about them truthfully in the light of his adulthood? There is something about childhood that makes it look with motives so different, with vision so much clearer and more imaginative than it will ever be again, after it has passed the invisible margin.

So in my childhood, my Aunt Maude seemed to me to be a rather wonderful person. She was different from any other people I knew; there was something in her spirit that seemed in a constant struggle with itself and with the world around it, and I could only watch its beatings with curious eyes and mind.

She was a tall large-boned woman, not beautiful, not even attractive, though her face was heart-shaped and rather delicate above her powerful body. But her hands were fine. They were large and plump and where the knuckles should have been were only tiny webs of wrinkles in the white skin. I liked to watch those hands, and even as they turned redder and coarser with each year's work, I still liked to watch them. It seemed as if something was being added through the years; a sort of

Four

....

character, a record of what great labor she undertook, what hard work she accomplished.

When she worked, she threw herself almost fanatically into the job, sparing nothing, regarding nothing, until it was done. Quarrel and fret she might during the whole time, but she did the job. I remember in the summers when she would do the week's washing in the morning, out on the old springhouse porch, she would do it all by hand, wringing and scrubbing until she was wet with perspiration. When the clothes hung white and flapping on the line, she seemed satisfied. But then, in a paroxysm of energy, she would throw herself into ironing that very afternoon. Coming in from the shade of the big black gum tree which stood in her yard, I would find her standing at the old ironing board, the steam rushing up from the iron and the clothes, the room hot and breathless.

"Good Lord!" she would say, when I asked her why she didn't wait, "It'll probably be hotter tomorrow, and besides, I wanted to get it over with."

She was always working to get the task at hand over with, as if, when all the menial work lay beyond her reach and out of the way, she might go on to that which she was really meant to do.

Above all, and blotting out the minor undercurrent of her frets and fumings, was her humor. Lusty bordering on the bawdy, her humor was like that of some Shakespearean character, perhaps Maria in *Twelfth Night*, which rushed forth to encompass anyone whom it met. She gave nicknames to anyone and everyone. One old woman in the valley, whose main delight was spreading rumor, she named "The Old Cat." And there was something like a cat about her wide face and spreading mouth, about the tiny whiskers that grew on her chin, that made the name at once ridiculous and fitting. Her grandfather she called "The Little Goat," and there again was the same ludicrous aptness. For he was small, and his beard and bright brown eyes did bear resemblance to those of a quick-eyed goat.

Of her own name she was particularly critical. "Out of all the names to choose from in this world, and me the first child, wouldn't you have thought Papa and Mama could have found something better than Maude? Just say it and you can picture some long raw-boned mountain woman like me. Good Lord, there are only two things I ever heard named Maude in my life. One is every old mule for fifty miles around in the country, and the other is me."

All during those years I knew her she was inescapably romantic. It is an ironical fact that being a romantic, she probably had less romance in her life than any other person I have ever known. There was an apple orchard of about two dozen trees in front of her house, and in the springtime when they bloomed, their fragrance and delicacy seemed almost to hurt her.

Have you ever seen an English apple orchard in the
    spring, in the spring,
An English apple orchard in the spring,
When the spreading trees are hoary with their wealth of
    promised glory,
And the mavis tells its story in the spring?

How many times I heard her say those lines over and over in a sort of rhythm that kept time with her work. And now and then she would look out to the trees loaded with white and pink, or walk under them in the early spring evening, her heavy old shoes making tracks in the damp earth.

Perhaps she was most romantic, however, when she played the piano. It was a reddish-stained upright which sat in the parlor. On top it wore a green velvet cover with tassels on the end and two piles of music Aunt Maude had had years before when she was teaching and could afford the luxuries of music. The room was ceiled, and stained with a dark brown color which bordered on the red of the piano. It was a gloomy room, dark and cold in the winter, dusty and unused in the summer, but the view from its windows was incomparable and stretched to

Four

range upon range of mountains in the distance. Then occasionally, when Aunt Maude played the piano, the room came to life. I can remember so vividly those still summer evenings when she would raise the windows in the parlor and the sound of her singing and playing would reach our house below and across the brook. It came, an indistinct and vaporous sound, like music, and yet like the sounds of water and the trees between. So I would go across and stand outside near the white spirea bush, or stand inside near the piano. Her hands drew music out of the keys swiftly and certainly. I, who could not play any instrument of music, watched the magic she wrought and listened to this language she spoke. A language which moved me but which I could not speak in answer.

"The Sheik of Araby," "In the Heart of a Fool," "Three O'Clock in the Morning"—those were the sentimental popular songs I recall, and she could sing them with as much feeling and enjoyment as any professional I have since heard. *The Golden Book of Favorite Songs* and *The Gray Book of Favorite Songs*, they were there. How many years had she played their pieces. Then there was semi-classical music, the operettas and the musicals she knew, and a bit of the classical—the more familiar classical. She had never had an opportunity to know the symphonies and operas, but those she had found she took to her repertoire, blending all the music she knew together in a happy pot-pourri of expression; the only means of expression which she had found.

The psychologists and psychiatrists today have given us names such as escapism and substitution, but I still prefer to call that quality in Aunt Maude by the name of romance—romance in a world where she had found little but the harshest realism. Her whole view of nature was so unlike my father's, or even my mother's, although they were sisters, that it interested me no little. There was a dark brooding superstition which overhung her whole response to the natural life around her. A patch of clover was possibly fragrant and lovely in its thick green leaves and white blossoms, but to her it became a search for a four-leafed clover. Sometimes she pretended it was just a game she played, but always underneath was the secret belief—and hope—that finding that bit of greenery with an extra leaf would bring her luck. The same was true for horseshoes, which she hung in various trees over her place, and even one in the house where it would not be seen. The first bluebird in spring was more than a symbol of the passing of the winter, a season which she hated; it was a sign of happiness, and she longed for it to nest in her trees. The year I was four she gave me a bracelet—a pretty little silver thing, and dangling from its two silver chains were tiny wrought bluebirds. "For luck," she said, and winked at me.

One night a screech owl came to a tree close beside Aunt Maude's windows and cried its mournful mysterious wail which is so unlike any screech. For days afterward, Aunt Maude was brooding and downcast. "It means death," she said. "Certainly some bad luck." But no death occurred. Then several months later, she was put to bed with a painful illness. "It was that damned screech owl," she triumphed. "I knew something bad was going to happen. And who else on God's earth but me would have ever thought of having a floating kidney dangling around somewhere inside of me!"

So her humor warred with superstition and made her so warm and human and colorful that I, for one, shall never forget her.

WINTER MORNING and tracks in the snow, running across the yard and disappearing in the thickness of laurel and rhododendron beyond. Something had come last night when we were asleep and passed silently over our grounds. Our grounds? How little did that ground belong to us. It was the bee's, the rabbit's, the fox's, the hundred plants' and insects' that had chosen to live upon it. How much more thoroughly did they know and possess this strip of common land, than we.

There were the tracks, fresh and dark against the whiteness of the fluffy unpacked snow. What had traveled abroad last

Four

....

31

night; where had it come from, where was it going, what was it seeking?

How I ached when I was a child with that longing which borders on desperation, to follow some such animal of the woods and know its life. To see what it saw last night and *as* it saw; to hear the rustle of the falling snow and be aware of other sharp bright eyes peering through the darkness—this was what I wanted to know. And perhaps it is because of such longing that children are permitted to bring their imaginations into the routine of everyday living. Not only do they seek for the facts, they seek for the "feel" of things. Our day has become a day of facts, a carnival of statistics, annotated biography, calculations in figures dealing with men, money, and machines.

I stood looking at the footprints in the snow.

"It's a rabbit's tracks," my father said.

That was the fact. My imagination surrounded it and soared beyond it. And my father's eyes—they too followed the tracks to the edge of the woods, and his imagination joined with mine.

five

....

SUMMER THE YEAR I was five. The valley had been dry and thirsty for weeks. "We need rain" was the password to every conversation, and I, too, thought of the dryness and watched the garden become dusty. The leaves of the plants were grey-colored with the dust, and the green corn leaves had begun to curl. "We won't have any potatoes at all," my father said. "Worst time for them to go without water; just as they're beginning to bloom." So I watched the little white potato flowers and wished that they would not come now but would wait a little while.

Farmers, real farmers, who do not farm only for what they can take from the land, are more dependent on the land—they are part of it. They regulate their whole life by the seasons, by the whims of the weather and soil, and can make no move without consulting some force beyond their own control. Every day they must feel their own inadequacy, for there is an intangible boundary beyond which their hopes and struggles will be of no use. Perhaps it is because of a dim realization of this fact that droughts and floods are accepted with the stoicism peculiar to these farmers.

But the dry spell did not continue. It had only suggested the possibilities of a drought when the rain began. The rain came quickly at first, as is the way of mountain showers in the summertime; they appear suddenly over the mountains, shower a heavy torrent of rain and then move on. But in the afternoon this rain decreased to a mild downpour. One of the pleasant downpours which children like, which lends a warmth and intimacy to the atmosphere of the house which is absent when the days are fair, and outside is as pleasant as in.

"The rain has slacked, but looks like it might be setting in for a while," Mother said.

It rained that night, the sound drowsy and distant against the roof, sweet to sleep by. The next morning it still rained, the drops larger and thicker, pouring like a veil between our house and the mountain opposite. Now certainly the dust was gone and the ground soaked, the rain could stop.

For almost a week, on and off, it rained, until the air was filled with wetness, until the fields stood in puddles, and the eroded hillsides down the valley were cut even more by the water which rolled over them and carried with it the best of the soil. Gutters were filled and overflowing, and the culverts along the road belched out great streams of water. The creek in front of our house had risen, higher and higher, until at last it swept over the embankments, down through a small orchard my father had planted, and over the bridge which led to our house. How queer it was to stand at the window and watch the water boil down over the planks of the bridge and swirl around the trunks of the apple trees. In the night we could hear great stones carried along by the current of the water, as they struck against each other and rushed down through the valley, rolling against the banks, tearing away lumps of the loosened earth. How small we felt, lying tucked in a tight little bed, while the water poured down through the valley outside our window and filled the night with the crashing strangeness of uprooted rocks. The whole world seemed to be in a chaos, a sudden wave and rush of movement, and we alone, lying inside the security of our house, were beyond its touch and reach. Safe we were, as the water ran through the orchard and pounded great stones together in a surge of energy.

But there were many who were not beyond its reach. I heard them talking of it later. Along the river which ran near the town, people abandoned their homes and watched the water carry them away, piece by piece, or whole and all at once. Chairs, chickens, stoves, hats—all the accumulated gadgets of eating and drinking, sleeping and dressing, and owning things in general, were swept together and carried away on the current of the river. When the rain stopped and we could go outdoors again, the world lay flat and beaten down around us. Everything was drenched, soaked to its capacity with water, and overflowing. The weaker plants lay along the ground, mingled with the heavy mud which spattered their leaves and stems. Tall, top-heavy flowers had fallen, too, and some had broken at the roots. There was the smell of water in the air, sweet, predominant over any other odor. It lent a subtle feeling of newness and fertility to the senses. Out in the orchard the water had fallen away and left behind it an almost solid layer of rocks. My small mind had not conceived that there might be so many rocks in the world. It was like the beginning of time, the beginning of the world. Wet and dark and shining they lay piled against one another, and in between was a sifting of sand, an occasional glisten of colored pebbles. I climbed among the rocks and picked up the red and yellow stones. They were prettier in the water. In my hand they dried and lost the sparkle of their newness.

During the morning the sun came out. Its brilliance dissolved through the mist but its warmth gradually dried the puddled ground and the trees. The rocks gave an indefinable odor of water and sun. The heat steamed against their hard surface, and they dried and settled in the places where the whirling flood had thrown them.

MY FATHER made me a swing in the maple tree in our yard. The ropes were long, for a limb strong enough to hold the swing and whatever weight it might have, had been a good distance from the ground. I have never known, before or since, a simple object which brought more real pleasure than that swing. The steel-made swings we had at school later were not nearly so good. They were hard, ugly devices which stood in the worn, sandy school yard behind the main building. But this swing was handmade, its seat was cut and shaped by hand, and below it was the grass and leaves, and directly above, the thick green maple leaves.

I gave myself wholly to the swinging, as children do. The body was free from tightness or inhibition, rising and falling and rising and falling in a rhythm of sweeping motion. Rising and falling . . . sometimes we stood, and then we could feel the wind and pressure of the resisting air against the length of body, rushing around us, almost through us with the heaviness of the impact. We would have stood with no clothes, so that the wind might strike our flesh, strike it hard and sharp and fall away as we rise and fall . . . rise and fall . . .

But then we liked the feel of the clothes, too—the follow and swirl as they whipped around our legs and stood wide before us like the billowing of sails . . . rising and falling.

Again, we did not stand in the swing, but sat, and then we could relax, the pumping made easier, and close our eyes and give ourselves over to the moment of pure ecstatic feeling. Rising and falling . . . rising and falling . . . this sheer body pleasure was a great good thing. On this we could use our animal energy. On this we could spend with utter recklessness the bounding end-less vital love of movement which surged within us. Vitality was in us, and we were in the moment. Then we would pump the swing with all our body, throwing ourselves forward into the air, dropping back upon the air, rising, falling . . . rising, falling . . . until the blood beat through our veins and pounded through our skin for release from the swiftness of the race. Our heart beat ter-rible and hard within our chest . . . then we would relax, and fall with the movement we had created, rising, falling . . . slower . . . slower. "Let the cat die down . . . "

And above, the sky was blue and liquid and the air was sweet around, and underneath the earth smelled warm of sun and age. In those times we felt as if we had touched some inner well of unknown earth-like vigor and cosmic energy. We had become alive.

Slower . . . slower . . . rising, falling . . . "Let the cat die down."

THERE IS a great deal of talk about realism. Perhaps it would seem to some that these first years of my life which I am speaking of are unreal, are somehow cradled in romanticism. I do not believe that any true realist, that is, one with imagination, can help also being a romantic. And, that is, a romantic in the noble sense of the word. My father was both realist and romantic. The first was of his head, the second of his heart. My mother was somewhat the same; she and my father followed the same path in the woods.

My half brother once sent us a popular novel when I was twelve, and I recall my father reading it.

"I didn't like it," he said at the end, with characteristic candor. "It is supposed to be realism, I guess. I've lived a pretty real life. The realistic life isn't like that, no matter where it's lived or by whom."

"What is realism, Daddy? Real realism," I asked, wanting the definition to use when I was reading books.

"Realism," he said, "is when you combine throwing cow manure on the pasture one hour and listening to the frogs and spring night sounds in the next hour, all in one chapter."

I did not try to defend or explain his definition. It stood alone. But I can state that in looking back over the very earliest years of my childhood, when memory is almost too dim to try to throw upon the screen, I find a juxtaposition of strange realities.

At this age of five and six, I am always somewhat surprised at how small a part people played in the life I remember. Psychologists may tell us otherwise, but for me then, existence in all its exciting forms was made up of objects. People merely played a role in the functional necessities of living. Eating, sleeping, dressing and undressing—all of these were eventful and to-be-looked-forward-to pleasures; but they were not the tremendous sparks that struck fire in my imagination and sent the bright flame blazing into a thousand different realms.

An unidentifiable hole in the ground, a bright pebble of many colors which lay at the bottom of the creek, an old piece of wire or box—these were the sorts of objects it took to make my mind

Five

leave its struggle for a grasp on the "realities" of life and go winging off into a world where any time and space was true. Since then, I have come to believe that this was more reality than the hum-drum commonplaces I was attempting to learn. Everyone sat in a high chair and learned not to spill the cereal in his spoon; everyone learned about his right shoe and his left and how to tie a bow knot. But how many were there, are there, that knew the depth of the reflections in our shallow pool, and how they formed an unknown dimension; or followed the way a chestnut burr fell to the ground with a little plop, and thus began to question the law of gravity so many books have explained so dully. Ah, which was the real world, which the imagined?

Yes, it was a world of objects, where each thing was new and somehow slightly incredible in its own uniqueness. But where is that sense of incredibility and uniqueness of things around us, where is it today? Can it be that somewhere between our second year and what is termed adulthood, we lose that Aladdin's lantern called imagination? It is indeed a magic lamp, for it throws a light which transforms all we see and know into a realm where past dreams and future results are more important than present facts. It transports the ordinary and the actual from a commonplace dullness into a realm of exciting possibilities. Imagination is not always, but usually, found in children. If they have not possessed too much, if they have not been coached by too many rules from the psychology books, if they have been allowed even a little freedom, there will be a spark of imagination. Surely imagination should be present in all artists and writers, for this is the morning spirit permitting them to speak and say what others cannot make articulate. But today it seems to be missing, in many writers especially, perhaps because I know the writers better. They have learned the rules and technique, they have followed the formulas, but where is the Aladdin's lantern which alone can throw the fire of talent, even genius, over the work? And in our living, in our eating, sleeping, working, entertainment—what have the automats and canned foods, the radio and movies, done to our imaginations? Imaginations which might provide us with an unbelievably natural and happy life, if we would but revive their powers. Have we truly, between childhood and maturity, lost this thing? Or have we failed to polish the Aladdin's lamp, failed to intensify its lustre, until now it lies far back in our memories, simply unused and tarnished?

Somewhat in relation to this, is the recollection of the pleasure I found as a child in doing things for the sake of themselves, as they came to hand. It might be opening a window, drying a plate, washing my face—but it could be imbued with all the imprisoned color of a prism of glass.

Today I perform these same duties, and other duties far more stimulating, but I do not always find the same animation I knew then long ago. Maybe it was because everything was new to me then. I had not opened so many windows or polished so many plates as I have now. But I believe it is rather because now, while I do these tasks, only half of me is there—the other half is worrying or planning or arranging some difficulty in the difficult world. I do not participate with freedom and wisdom as I once did. The old color and magic are gone.

What did we do that made it so different then? I think I felt all that I touched, felt it through my skin and down to the marrow of my bones. I saw what I looked at, lacking the preoccupation of duties which hang heavy now. I sensed implications in all that I did. Now perhaps, I would be afraid of conceit if I allowed myself to feel so important in the universe? How small a thing would be our fear of self-conceit if we could recapture the individual importance we once knew; an importance not so much of self, but of life. A trivial act, broadened to universal proportions, became suggestive of so much more than it in itself really was. It gave a sense of universality that only the great races of earth have ever known. If we could learn today the secret of recapturing, unashamed, the tangents between ourselves and the universe about us, who can dream of the greatness which would come alive in each of us, the nobility which would enter into our civilization,

Five

....

the future toward which we might hope? In that moment, breathless, we might reach out and touch the god within ourselves.

SOMETIME DURING the summer, he would come around to see us. In fact, he came to see everyone in the community. We called him The Preacher, and everyone knew who we meant, though he had not been a preacher in the little frame church for many years. He had been one of the first men to hold a pastorate in the community, and he had grown to know every family and every member of each family—what they did, who they married, how many children they had. As long as I had ever heard of him, which began when I was very small, he had lived in the eastern part of the state. His family had been well-to-do, he had been well educated for a man of his time, and he was now living in comparative comfort on a typical old plantation. His interest seemed never to wane in his old community, however, for he was in his seventies when I remember him. And when he came around, he walked every step of the way.

We would look out of the window and see him coming up to the road, usually in August when the sun was hottest and walking would seem most difficult. He always wore exactly the same thing: a long black frock coat and black trousers to match of the blackest material I have ever seen. They were of beautiful material and well made. His shirt always had a starched front, and in spite of the heat or sun his collar was never the slightest bit withered or wilted looking. When he reached our porch, he would remove his black silk hat and with an ample crisp white handkerchief slowly wipe the pin-point beads of perspiration off of his forehead and chin. He sat in the chair, caught his breath for a moment, and waited for his large body to be comfortable. He was a tall man with a broad chest and a physique that gave him an air of importance and significance. Perhaps all those qualities were sharpened because I saw him from my own small proportions. But there was certainly a largeness about him, a dignity of carriage and a sombreness of dress that impressed itself upon my mind. The queerest part was that his black shoes never seemed to be dusty or scarred by the rocks he had walked through. They shone as if he had only just polished them, and I—who was always battering my shoes and needing a polish— wondered about his technique and would have given much for the secret. But then, as I say, it might have been that after all he was not so perfectly groomed, but only seemed so to me.

After he had cooled and rested, he talked with us, always in the same manner, about the new people whom he had met in the house next door, about someone else's baby, or another person's son who had gone away and married. He questioned us too, remembering with remarkable accuracy names and dates and events. Oddly enough, I do not remember my father ever talking with The Preacher. I'm sure he must have, for he was the sort of person from whom my father would have learned the history of the community. But then again, they were at such opposite poles of character that perhaps there would have been little in common for them.

When The Preacher talked, he engaged in a minor struggle with his false teeth. I think he must have had two sets of false teeth, both upper and lower, and that each set was waging a battle to exchange places with the other set. When he opened his mouth to speak, he was at once forced to clamp his jaws together in order to keep the teeth in place. So the sentences would continue, words popping out in the moments between his dental activities. This gave a peculiar flavor of suspense to any conversation with him, and although the teeth never actually won and dropped in his lap as they seemed to wish to do, there were moments when victory on their side seemed imminent. On the whole, it was a noisy, inconvenient style of speaking, and why he did not get for himself a set of teeth that would fit, I do not know. Certainly he had the money and plenty of reason for exchange!

Usually he preached one sermon at the church before he left the valley, and then the problem of his speaking was crucial. With great bites on the air he would clamp his teeth together,

Five

and while they rattled back into place, he would draw a heavy breath in his lungs for the renewed attempt at speaking.

The Preacher had been married three times. "Yes," he would say, "I married three times. And every time I married a different sort. I've tried 'em all. The first time I married a pretty little girl, and I lived with her sixteen years and then she died. Now the next time, I married a red-headed widow and I lived with her twenty-five years. Then she died, too. And the last time I married a rich old maid. Well, she's still with me."

I would remember, for days after, the long emphasis he gave to each phrase: a pre-tty little girl, a red-headed widow, and a rich old maid. They made a tune, a sing-song verse.

So he would sit with us fifteen, twenty minutes, then gather his cane and hat and handkerchief and walk down the steps. His hat sat firmly on his head, tilting slightly toward the back, and he grasped his stick tightly in his hand. With a long breath and a final clamp on his loose teeth, he would say good-bye. We could hear him singing as he went down the driveway and turned into the road. Softly and indistinctly the words would float back to us—or usually to me alone, as I sat on the steps watching him go up the road:

There's a land that is fairer than day,
And by faith we can see it a-far;
For the Father waits over the way,
To prepare us a dwelling-place there.
In the sweet—by and by—
We shall meet — — —

THERE WERE long mornings when I could spend time freely, watching a crayfish among the water-soaked leaves and rocks, feeling as satisfied and worthy in the watching as if I had built something in wood and cement for everyone to see and consider.

There must always be something in everyone's memory that is symbolic of the mysteries he will never be able to explain, that stands for the unununderstandable things in life. For me, it was the stream in front of our house which was to remain as the forever mysterious. In spring, when the snow and ice had gone and the collected leaves along the banks lay heavy from the fall before, the water was swift and musical. It carried the odor of springtime and was the very heart of the newly stirred earth which lay on either side of it. Just below our bridge was a fine wide rock where I could sit for hours at a time and study the passage of the water, the stones, the leaves, the ferns. And just above the bridge was a mass of trees and undergrowth. In the spring, there was a spicewood there that bloomed almost as soon as the water itself had begun to flow with the new-found spirit. Later, there was rhododendron, white and pink, which bloomed in stiff nosegay clusters above the green bedding of leaves. When the blossoms began to fade, the petals would often fall off into the water, where they were floated on down to me, and past me, as I waited on the rock. There was a little eddy beside the rock where some of the petals would become marooned and lie there turning brown among the browner leaves.

Of course in the summer I waded in the creek. The sand and stones were sharp against my feet, but there was always pleasure in an unexpected deep place where the water might rise around my knees. The greatest fun came from sitting on the rock, with feet and toes bobbing in and out of the water, and simply smelling the sun on one wet arm and watching a lizard slither out between the leaves or a crayfish crawl from under a stone.

The winter was the most beautiful season of them all. Then the water ran dark and cold between icy crusts along the bank, and there was some haunting quality about the sight and sound which made me look for long moments without pause along the crooked winding creek below where the water ran away from me, and into the shadowy darkness of laurel and rhododendron above, where the water ran toward me. If it had snowed, then the creek was usually the only sound in the air. Under the bridge, along the big log underpinnings, icicles hung, slender and clear. Sometimes they had formed around the roots and

Five

ferns or mosses which grew alongside; there in the center of the frozen ice would be a root-thread of life visible, encased in a voluntary seal. It was like the ages past, when the earth was in formation and ice lay like a blanket over the surface of all things.

These ferns and mosses came into their rightful domination during the winter. Flowers were long since dead, and leaves lay rotting all around, but these green things remained as beautiful as ever. Perhaps even more beautiful. For the cold air and freezing snow seemed to have freshened the green and made it free from the dust of summer. Most of the ferns were the stocky-leaved, sturdier kind that grew near the ground and did not attempt a show like the larger ferns which grew behind our house. There was one variety of moss which was colored a particularly brilliant green. It was so bright that any little piece of it along the bank was enough to liven up the whole view.

Then there were the other mosses, which grew flat and hard, or soft and cushiony, and ranged through many shades of yellow-green and blue-green. They soaked the melting ice and snow, and in the summer their roots would hold the water for many days of dryness, providing the roots of shrubs and trees with needed moisture. It seemed that everything in nature had its purpose.

So the creek played a subtle part in those early days. We have often heard life compared with the flowing ceaselessness of a river. My life always seemed more like the bed of a creek, the bed which remains fairly constant through the years while a stream of physical, mental, and emotional events flowed swiftly by on its surface. At bedrock, the sand shifted only slightly under the rush of this water, under the reflections of sun and shadow, leaf and limb, which varied vaguely; all while the stream had risen or fallen in its depth but had incessantly flowed on down the hill.

BUILDING A FIRE is a task of gentleness and faith and skill. People who have had no experience go about the beginnings of a fire with too much energy, too much determination to make it burn in spite of itself. They are like the traditional nouveau riche, they think that quantity can replace quality. This is never true with kindling. They think that forceful bluster can serve as well as patience and care, which is never true with a fire. In short, it is a work of art.

Also, this was one of the things in which my mother excelled over my father.

"Bonnie's the best hand to build a fire I ever saw," I can remember him saying.

There was something about the way she could crumple a piece of paper, lay a few splinters of wood across, and strike a match, that made the flames curl directly around the kindling, then around the logs, and finally resolve into a blazing fire. Or sometimes she could come into the room when the fireplace had been smoking, and by her shifting of one of the logs, by a push with the poker here, or a touch there, the smoke would suddenly gather itself together and drift up the dark throat of the chimney as it was meant to do.

The odors of the wood we burned brought particular happiness to mother. Green wood with sap bubbling out of the ends, or heavy rosinol pine. Once I remember we found an old pine stump in the woods, and she pulled off bits of the jagged edges.

"Look how rich it is," she said. "It will fill the whole room with the smell of pine when it burns." And her eyes were brown and shining as new-peeled chestnuts.

Later, much later, when we had lived a winter together in a large city and had known but little except the gray smoke of coal, I remember walking in a suburb one snowy evening, when suddenly she stopped.

"Smell," she said, scarcely above a whisper.

It was the unmistakable odor of wood smoke, pungent, familiar across the cold night air as an old pair of bedroom shoes. Mother stood still, breathing deep the sweet and bitter smell she knew as well as any smell on earth. Her face was bright with recognition and nostalgia.

Five

....

45

There is the sound of a fire, which is good too. I cannot imagine what people have missed who never dreamed before a hissing steaming set of logs, who never watched the blue spurting darts of strange little flames, or never heard the mutterings of discontented wood burning swiftly in the night. And as they listened, never wondered at this unknown infinitesimal world of sound. To have missed the singing of wood when you were a child is to have missed a whole area of imagination. And if you missed, too, the colors of fire, the shapes of figures in the flames, and in the burning coals, then you will never understand the meaning which a fireplace and an open fire can hold for some of us who knew them in our childhood nights.

It is all these things which enter into the building of a blazing fire: the memories of other fires before, the feel of wood, the smell of smoke.

THE FIRST SNOW that year came in October. It was a surprise that came overnight and transformed the whole world. We were in the midst of a season, we had found something that seemed certain and lasting for awhile—then suddenly the scene was shifted and we, the mere spectators, were left a little stunned. That was the way of it that year.

Fall had come to the mountains, and the trees stood bright and challenging in a range of color. The oaks were their own dark red, so utilitarian, so persistent after the gaudier leaves had fallen. Maples red, orange, chestnuts brown and yellow, and the broad yellow of poplar leaves. We reveled in the stimulus of so much brilliancy and relaxed in the mystical haze which hung over the hills, softening the colors and spreading over our spirits a deep sense of sadness and nostalgia. By October the mountains had reached their zenith. Then the snow came. Came suddenly, came lightly—blew its white breath along the valley, up the mountains, left behind an unbelievable sort of world.

The color remained as it had been, for how in one brief night and day could it eliminate or adjust itself. But on top of each leaf lay a cover of white. Like some protecting sheet of material, pure white had drawn up over the russets and reds and yellows as if to subdue their brazenness and bring to the trees instead a virginal modesty. But who can describe such moments of nature? Who can attempt to carve little words to fit the frame of the picture and find them not grow pale in his very hands beside the reality of the memory he bears in his mind? These are the moments when truth seems farthest, when the very differences between the attempted likeness and the real subject are so great as to make an actual lie out of the likeness. But the world, nevertheless, was an incredible sight; it took your breath away, as the saying is, and that was so. The leaves were still so large and thick, the foliage of weeds and flowers had not even fallen, and each barren and acquiescent space had been covered with the snow. The bark of the trees looked dark and shiny underneath, as if a glow of health permeated from the falling sap through the dark roughness of the skin. Even the crackling leaves on the ground had been covered, and were silent.

The heaviness was what most impressed, however. Coming when it had, the snow had added its weight to the limbs, and the leaves themselves had provided larger receptacles for the snow, until the trees were burdened by an unaccustomed weight. Limbs curved gracefully toward the ground, each twig felt the pressure of new weight and bent under the load. Top-heavy trees leaned toward the side, until some of the snow slipped along the branches and fell shattering to the ground.

When the limbs began to break, we could hear them first far up on the mountainside. A splitting sound of something torn apart, and then a crash as the limbs fell to the ground. It sounded mysterious and far away, those distant echoes on the mountains. Watching, we could sometimes see a speck of movement. They were distant and did not concern us, only the sounds and sight penetrated to us. But the breaking began to happen nearer by, and we became more interested. Two great

Five

....

47

branches tore loose from oak trees in the yard. One of the trees was to bear the scar the rest of its life.

As they fell close-by, how loud the sound came, how still the silence afterward. I sat in our living room by the fireplace or at the window and memorized the colors and the snow, eyes bright with the dark mysterious sounds of crashing limbs and trees, rendering scars which were to last long after the snow had been forgotten.

six

....

IT WAS JULY the year I was six years old that the
man came into our yard and gave us a foretaste
of the years which were to come. My father was
working in the ground beside the rows of pines
he had planted, when the stranger came up the driveway. He
had parked his bright new-model car in front of our gate and
was walking gingerly over our bridge. He came even more gingerly along the gravel, then stepped off onto the clipped grass.
His shoes were shiny like the car, sporty brown and white they
were. I remember because they were the first brown and white
shoes I had seen.

My father pulled his garden trowel out of the ground and
watched the man.

"Nice place you have here," the newcomer said.

"Thank you. I like it," Daddy replied.

Mother and I watched them standing there talking. Then we
went toward them and my father introduced Mother and the
man. The three of them stood a moment, then the man said,
"I just asked your husband here how much he'd take for his
place."

Mother did not move. She simply stood, silent, as if she could
not realize what he had said. Always her home meant more to
her than to anyone else I ever knew. Sell it? Move out? Where
would they go? They had only begun to fix it as they really
wanted it. Her home—this man wanting to buy it. Could he be
serious? He didn't look like the type to . . .

....

"Oh I don't want it for a place of my own," the man laughed, seeming to catch Mother's unasked question. "You see, I have some out-of-town clients, and I think they'd like this place." He turned to Daddy again. "I really must be in a hurry though as I have an appointment in town. I just happened to drive by this place on the way to the orchard. How much will you take for it?"

My father named a sum. I did not know how much it meant, but I could see that my mother was incredulous at the amount. The man did not seem surprised or thrown off balance in any way.

"Fine," he said. "I'll see you tomorrow." And he turned to leave. Mother looked at Daddy. How could he have asked that much, what had he been thinking of?

The man stopped in the driveway, and now he called, "Don't let anyone else have a bid on it before I see you again."

My father smiled. "Another optimistic real estate agent," he said when the man had driven away in his green car.

"But so much," Mother said, "you told him so much for it."

"That's the only thing I'd sell it for," Daddy answered her. "He asked me what I wanted if I should sell, and I told him. Would you want to sell for less?"

"No-o," Mother said.

"Don't worry. He won't be back. I know. I've seen men like him before. Wild dreams, no foundation." And Daddy went back to the work with his trowel.

But that was one time when he was mistaken. The man did come back, and the next afternoon, too. He brought a couple with him. The woman was short and had bright eyes which smiled easily. Her husband was a tubercular. They walked over our garden, our lawn, and through the house. It seemed unnatural to have these strange people looking with such critical eyes at our place and our home. Before they left, the real estate man took my father aside. "They like it," he said. "I told them your price."

The next day he brought a contract with him, and within the week our house was sold. With what incredible swiftness had the course of our life been swerved into another channel.

That was at the very edge, the horizon-beginning, of the boom. The Boom! Those years when people spent money like water through a sieve, when land became real only on paper, and acres which never even existed were bought and sold and traded. Asheville during the boom was an incredible city. It, if any city, might well have been called the city of dreams. Soap-bubbles, air castles. The people had had a taste of the luxurious life, an inkling of what money could bring, in the estate which George Vanderbilt had built in their midst. A fabulous home built on the model of the Chateau at Blois, it had outdone everything that might be built in Asheville again, and yet it had created, in the most modest-salaried families, a taste for things above their reach. It was as if they had drunk of the rare vintage wine and would never be satisfied again with their home corn-licker.

This did not start the boom in Asheville; it was merely a taste and a craving which spurred it on to even more ridiculous heights than it might have reached otherwise. There was a great combination of things which started that boom—things which were present all over the country. The economists have tried to explain them to us. At any rate, whatever the reasons, the boom came. And insofar as we were concerned, it came to us the day a stranger in a sporty white suit came in our yard and accepted our home for a price we had not imagined he would take. How soon were homes all over Asheville to be sold in that manner, the prices going higher and still higher with every new sale, until people—the sellers and the buyers too—were so drunk on figures that an extra zero, or two, meant little on the contract. Our boom was tied in closely with the Florida boom. Speculation progressed in much the same degree in both places, and those who had become rich overnight in Florida came here to find more wealth, and the same happened with our own speculators, who felt that newer and broader fields were to be had in the sunshine state.

I recall so much of it vaguely, yet how clear are the conversations in which people were arguing with my father about his money.

"Why don't you invest it, Dykeman?"

"I intend to. In a home."

"Yes, yes. But you can build that on time payments. I mean invest your money in more real estate—several pieces—why, you don't know how much you might make. We're really going places in this town. I'd advise you to invest it and make a good neat profit."

"Thanks. I'll get my own place first."

Or again, when one of the stout-stomached, merry little men from the town was speaking with him:

"Now look here, Mr. Dykeman, I'm telling you this for your own good."

Raised eyebrows, on my father's part.

"Oh, I'll get a commission out of what sales I make, yeah, but what's that? Chicken feed. I could be making twice as much in my own office right now. But I want to see you in on a good thing. And be-lieve you me, we've got it here. This place's going to see a rise in the tide like it's never seen before. And it's going to be the fellers like you an' me who were in on the ground floor that make the hauls!"

"You mean you think we're going to have new residents?"

"New residents?" The man looked incredulous. "New residents! Lord, man, this place is already swarming with people who have just come here to live. Can't find places to tuck 'em all. New residents? Why, the way people are going to come pouring in here when our Chamber of Commerce gets to work is going to be somethin' to make the census takers start rubbin' their bunions."

And the Chamber of Commerce did go to work. Every new development was written up with greater gusto than the one before. Each little suburb was to become a haven for wealthy outsiders, and little cottages and staked-off lots sprang into being overnight. The phrase of "those wealthy New Yorkers" was constantly heard, for the old idea seemed to remain, and still does, that everyone from New York was wealthy and should be treated with the deference due to that estate.

Six

....

Pieces of paper became more real than homes, and riches were made and lost in the flourish of a pen along those pieces of paper. Things moved so rapidly that those in the current could not possibly have paused a moment to take stock of themselves. Everything was bought on margin. A few dollars would give ownership to an entire lot in one of the newest developments, a few more dollars would give a shared interest in a new venture which was in turn to make all the investors millionaires overnight. So what funds people had were divided up, dribbled into a dozen pools, until they owned parts in a dozen "good things," and all of nothing.

As I say, people could not understand my father's ability to sit back and watch others grow rich without himself participating in the spoils. They gave him advice who had always asked it before, they gave him "good tips" who had tried to borrow money from him in the past. He saw some of the men in the town grow rich and attain a long car for every member in their family. We still had our old Dodge.

"We can't let our car get bigger than we are," Daddy said, with an odd smile, when I wondered about our getting a new one. "That wouldn't do, would it little girl?" he said.

So the years of the later 1920s slipped away, and the thirties approached. Each year, the heights of Asheville finance had become a little dizzier. We had built another home and moved in, had gone on a western trip which we would never forget, and had lived in our same simple manner through those years. The orgy of spending was reaching its climax.

"Sometime," my father said, "we'll find out that we've put too much effort in business and not enough on studying things out."

Then the climax came, and with a reverberating crescendo, the fall from glory began.

One morning, Mother and I were on our way to town and stopped at a neighbor's house. She greeted us at the door with her eyes staring wide and her apron whipping in the wind about her. "The bank's busted wide open," she cried. And that was that.

How funny that sentence seems now, on paper, upon recalling the disheveled state of that woman's appearance and bearing. Then, it was something like a bomb-shell. We could not even comprehend what it meant for a few moments after her unheralded outburst.

When we reached town, a line of people stood before the closed doors of the bank building, and other people milled around in noisy groups. How queer it seemed to see those doors closed on a week-day morning. I could remember all the times I had been inside and stood beside the white marble counters, wondering when I would be high enough to see over the top. I could remember the dark mouth of the vault which stood at the back of the long room, and the iron grillwork which covered that mouth; the low, efficient voices of the tellers as they spoke with Mother or Daddy about something or counted out bills for them; the shininess of it all—the glistening marble, the spittoons, the clear tall windows. Now it was closed and locked.

People in the crowd spoke with one another, and there was confused disbelief in their eyes. This could not have happened to them. They had been so safe. They had been so secure. Those who had had much, those who had had little—all refused to believe what had happened to them. Funny things occurred too. They were funny later, but not at the time. At the time, they were tragic. Like the one old mountain fellow who pushed through the crowd and rushed against the door. The tobacco juice flew from his mouth.

"By God, they've got to lemme in. I've got eighty-seven dollars of 'baccer money in thar. If'n they don't let me in, an' quick, I'll sue 'em fer hit. Yessir, by God, fer every last'n cent o' hit." No one could laugh at his tragic earnestness, for they, too, had pounded on the door and whispered silently to themselves the same words.

We did not stay in town but went home to tell my father the news. He was serious and grave. And yet, somehow, there was something which had been present in that crowd of people which he did not have. The hysteria, the panic, were missing.

"What will we do?" Mother cried, and she could not keep from crying, as so many others were crying in so many other homes.

"We'll get along," he said, as so many men years younger than he had failed to say.

I crept upstairs and went into the closet. I can still taste those lonesome tears I cried. My little savings had been in that bank, and I realized that they had been taken too. Mother found me in the closet and she called Daddy.

"Wilma's been crying," she said to him. "Her savings are gone too, I guess. We'd forgotten about that."

She and Daddy looked at each other. I realized something was passing between them which I did not understand.

"Now look here," Daddy said, and his tone was very quiet, "there's to be no more crying over money in this house. We'll get along."

And that was the end of our panic. What came after, the closing of other Asheville banks, the suicides, the beginnings of the depression, did not matter, for our panic had been over long before. It had been short lived.

This was not so for the majority of Asheville, however. Despair rushed like a wave over the city. (Men jumped out of windows, and wives followed their husbands everywhere they went because of the dark threat of suicide which hung potent in the air.) The paper became one great obituary notice, and the main city graveyard had a suicide plot. With razors, from windows, by bullets, the men of fortune ended the whirling gyrations which had caught them up and carried them along to ruin. There was something appalling about their utter helplessness before the situation. What utter defeat they must have felt to have figured that death could solve its riddle better than life. The flimsiness of the scaffolding they had pinned to was made all too apparent. A doubt, a questioning, a turning of the eyes inward, engrossed the people who were left to live.

As it was with us, our lives had been simple, and we did not find it difficult to simplify more. Indeed, perhaps we liked it

Six

....

just as well. What income my father had not had swept away from him had been frozen or depleted. Yet I do not recall great fears and hardships during those difficult years. Perhaps it was because I could not recall such superfluous luxuries and desires during the easier years. Then, we were lucky to have our home and our place. I am glad now that my father and mother had not spent the money they had in the bank. "Might as well have spent it," people said, "you lost it anyway." That was not the point. If we had spent it in the frenzied likeness of so many others, how much more our appetite for things would have grown—we would have needed so much more to make us happy. As it was, we had had what we needed and some more besides. And now we were not hungry for something bigger and better and shinier all the time; and we controlled our money—it did not control us.

"My stars!" Daddy would say, as he read through the paper and smoked his ever-present pipe, "who would have thought it." Who would have thought it indeed! The years had rolled too swiftly and the momentum was suddenly blocked; action had gripped the spotlight and movement was all that had mattered— and suddenly thought had stepped in and forced recognition of itself.

It is so, that when we are brought up short for a moment in our circle of activity, when we suddenly lose or find ourselves mistaken in some big plan, we must fall back on what is inside of us. It is the ultimate proof that the only real life we can live is the life which goes on in the tiny space within our skulls. Mind and spirit are what eventually save us from ourselves. They are what we possess without benefit of money or manipulation; they are the links between us and the rest of the universe. They open the door to the only relationship where man can fulfill his destiny— the relationship between his humanity and his godliness.

THE WINTER AFTER we sold our house and moved to the new place where we were going to build another home, we lived in a three-room attachment to our garage which was to become later my father's workshop. It was while we were living there that my mother was ill with the intestinal flu.

I was six years old and it was the month of March when she was sickest. March in the mountains can be a treacherous month, for it brings the unexpected, and that year the unexpected was the bitterly cold weather. At the beginning of her illness our bedroom had been upstairs in a large unceiled room, but we moved her downstairs soon, and the bed seemed out of place in the living room. I felt very far away and removed from their world when I went upstairs now, for I still slept in my little bed up there, and everyone else was downstairs. There was no one to talk to after I lay in bed; there was only cold and fright.

I was afraid my mother would die. Lying in the darkness, I would hear the doctor's voice below, for he sometimes came at night, and an indistinct murmur of his voice, blended with my father's, floated up to me. I could not tell what they were saying, and yet I knew they were talking; I could not tell what they were doing and yet I heard them moving about below me. It was the fear of blindness and not knowing that clutched me. There were long silences when I wondered what the doctor was doing, when I would bury my head in the covers and count, slowly, to a hundred, so that he might have time to finish the silence and when I listened again I might hear him speaking.

Such are the fears that obsess a child when he senses the situations and yet has no knowledge with which to meet them; when he realizes the possibilities and is yet kept from participating in the moment by moment elimination of those possibilities. Strange afterwards, too, to look back on the unhappy period and realize what a queer little lot of things you remember. There was a checked blue and white pillowcase I had for my small-sized pillow which I shall not forget, nor the smell it had, cold against my cheek when I first crawled in bed at night. Too, there was a little book of advertisement put out by a nose-drop firm [Vick's] which told the tale of two little elves named Blix and Blee. I wonder if anyone else ever saw that booklet; it was more memorable to me than most of the "good" children's books I read. Something about it caught my fancy, maybe the illustrations, and I read it over to myself, and to Mother as she lay in bed, and to the dark, when I lay alone and could not tell what the voices below were saying.

I suppose the strangest thing of all was having Mother sick. I believe it was the first time I had ever seen her ill since I had come on this earth, and it was a fairly startling experience. It is the same experience everyone goes through the first time his mother is sick, and he must find all the little trifles she has always found for him before; and most of all he must walk through a lonesome house.

After a while there was medicine to be given regularly to Mother, at intervals through the night.

"You must not forget this now," the doctor said, "and oversleep, for she must have the medicine, and on time."

"I won't forget," my father said.

And he didn't. Sometimes I would hear him during those nights, sometimes not, when he turned on the light and found the spoon and medicine. There was always the faint click of the glass bottle-edge against the spoon, then the click as he twisted the top back on the bottle. Sometimes he had to speak to Mother to rouse her attention to him, then his hushed voice and her weak one would break the little pattern of sounds. Soon the springs downstairs would murmur as my father again gave them his weight, and the click of the light switch would erase the hundred cracks of light which had filtered from the lower room through the floor where I slept. Now the brief contact with those below me had vanished, and I was alone, the wind rushing near the eaves of my room, and the creaks and noises of the wood all around seemed very near and real. I could go to sleep though, because there had been the voices downstairs, and I felt ungrateful to be afraid when Mother had been so ill and so much worse might have happened to us all.

It is that first contact with great sickness, that first contact with the doctor and his invariable leather bag, which makes a child fear death. It makes him remember the night noises which were around him, the subdued voices he could not understand, and the pale cracks of light which broke up the darkness in the lonely room.

ONE OF THE STRANGEST plants I ever found in the woods I came across one day in June on our new place. I was walking through a remote part of our woods, where I had seldom been before, and where the undergrowth was thick and dark. The rhododendron leaves were particularly green, almost as if there had been some black mixed in the coloring. In a little open space I came across a group of plants which were unfamiliar to me. I had never seen them before. Later I found out that they were called Indian peace pipes, or just Indian pipes.

Standing there in the shaded darkness, they looked like the ghosts of real plants; like the mummified images of flowers dead long ago. For they were a peculiar white shade, a dead white, one might say, and there was no trace of color about them. They stood from two or three inches to seven or eight inches tall, and bore no leaves—only, perhaps, the beginnings of leaves, or scars where leaves might have been at one time in another stage of development. At the end grew a single flower, and it was exactly in the shape of a pipe bowl, hanging with head down and all the stiff white petals forming a small round cup. Around the cluster of pipes grew several tall green ferns, their brilliant greenness merely emphasizing the whiteness of the strange plants. The rotting leaves were thick and damp underfoot, providing the richness of the soil which Indian pipes require.

These Indian pipes fall under the division of organic life called saprophytes. They live off of the dead in the rest of the organic world, either plants or animals. No wonder that their whiteness is so startling, so unnatural. They do not possess the magic chlorophyll which gives the greenness to other plant life and permits it, through contact with the sun, to manufacture its own life-food. They are forced to live off of the compounds

Six

....

59

which are present in dead animals and plants. As they slowly reduce these compounds to their own use, they cause the decay of the object they have fastened upon. So the cycle of life feasting on death revolves, and these waxy, fragile plants come into their own.

I was caught by the unearthly quality of these plants I had found. I decided to take one home with me to find out more about it. So I knelt down by the bed and picked one of the long smooth specimens. It felt clammy, like a bloodless finger. As I carried it home, a slow transformation seemed to take place in its appearance, and I suddenly realized it was turning black. By the time I had finished my walk, the plant was dark and discolored; all the waxy whiteness had disappeared.

Since then, I have never come across Indian pipes growing in the woods without wondering at their ethereal delicacy. Somehow, they are neither plant nor flower, but a peculiar incarnation of the weird unearthly portions of the woods.

AN ELECTRIC STOVE can never replace a wood range. Admitted, it is quicker, cleaner, more efficient; but where is the red glow and the smell of burning wood and the warmth?

Our wood stove, as most, had a thermometer on the oven door which could register the heat for purposes of baking. The sight of that thermometer and the sound of the springs on the oven door as they whined when the door was opened or closed, these became associated in my mind with the smell of chocolate cake and spicy apple butter in the making. I recall one cold night when I had been outside and came into the kitchen directly from the outside air. None of the lights had been turned on, although it was growing dark fast, and the cracks around the stove lids and the firebox door gave forth a yellow luminousness; the glow was reflected on the walls and flickered though the shadows. And added to this, was that odor of apple butter. It filled the room as completely as a tangible thing, it was so pungent and so real that it seemed as if I could reach out and touch it, hold it in my hand. I stood at the door, stretching out the moment. Mother came into the room. She did not see me, where I stood in the shadow of the door. I watched her as she went to the stove and, opening the oven, drew forth the two wide pans of russet-colored stuff. Now the odor must certainly be there to grasp—it was so warm and heavy. Mother took a long wooden spoon from the table and slowly, with winding movements, stirred the apple butter. It clung and dripped, giving off little waves of steam when the spoon sank into it. Then she laid the spoon aside, took the blue and white pot-holder in her hand and pushed the pans back into the darkness and heat of the oven. She closed the door, then came and switched on the light. I had hardly realized I was watching her. All of her movements had been so swift, so easy, it might have been that I was watching a shadow-show, like in the figures people make with their hands thrown into the shadow along the wall. There is a curious satisfaction in watching someone who is unaware of your presence. It is a sense of omnipotence, perhaps, of seeing something by accident, some personal moment you were not meant or intended to see. So it had been with this. Now, in the light, I came back to myself. I wondered why Mother had not switched on the light at first. "I liked the evening," she said. "I hated to let it go before I had to. . . . The apple butter will soon be done."

There are times like that—in a kitchen, in the woods, in a crowd of people, it doesn't matter where—when some secret exultation or joy comes up in you and immortalizes the moment. Those are the moments you can't tell of on paper because they aren't a story or a narrative; they're a feeling, an essence, a communion.

Then there is the warmer on a range. An electric stove has nothing comparable to that, so far as I know. It was the place where the heat was gradual and mild, where plates and platters could be heated, where food could be kept warm. Coming home from school, there was joy on looking in the warmer and finding

Six

some warm morsel to ease a hungry stomach until supper. And during the time when mother made her bread, the warmer became glorified; it was the stage for a little miracle which was taking place inside the long loaf pans. Its function was the slow warming of the dough, the rising of the kneaded loaves. Now it was as essential a part of the stove as any other, and had a function it alone could perform. There was something pleasing in this fact.

In summer, they say, the ranges are too hot; they turn the women into drudges. Perhaps it is because we lived in the mountains where the mornings and the evenings were usually cool and brisk, but a range was somehow good in summer too. In the early morning, which is the best part of a summer day, it took the dewy chilliness off the air, and though there are those who disagree with all work and all unpleasantness, there is something natural about heat when canning season comes. My mother never canned much—a little grape juice, a few jellies, some fruits, and maybe tomatoes for our use—but there seemed to be something right and in place in the flushed face and warm scented air of canning season. Not heat enough to oppress or stifle the body, but heat enough to make the cool of the evening a happy contrast to the day.

Now in our kitchen at home there stands a shining white electric affair, and certainly it is pleasant and simple to use. But there is also something gone, something which went when the wood range was taken.

Wilma and her father on the back steps of her birthplace, about 1922.

Ten-year-old Wilma in July of 1930 with her parents,
Bonnie Cole and Willard Dykeman.

Wilma's birthplace in Lynn Cove at the head of Beaverdam Valley. The log house was built by her parents in 1917.

Wilma on her fourteenth birthday (May 20, 1934) with her father, who died twelve days later.

Wilma, her parents, and her much older half sister, Helen Dykeman, celebrating the construction of the house built in 1926 just upstream from Wilma's birthplace.

Wilma Dykeman in January of 1943, less than two years before she began to write Family of Earth.

seven

I WAS SEVEN when I started to school. I had gone to kindergarten before, but that was only for a few hours in the morning. Real school was much different. I went on a school bus, a tan and brown affair the color of an old football, and with its squat sides, shaped much like a football. Before this, Mother, or one of the mothers of the girls going to kindergarten with me, had taken me in her car. Now I carried my lunch in a little square blue tin; before, I had been home for dinner.

The first day of school in the fall, from my first grade through college, never failed to arouse in me a feeling of excitement. But that very first day—how much more exciting it was than any other could ever be. All the impressions that were to come later were heightened and made manifold in those few hours, until the red brick building seemed gigantic, the halls stood long and endless, and on either side opened doors into classrooms which held unimaginable facts and information. In my own first room, there were six long tables, worn and hacked at the edges by others who had been there before. Around them were placed small chairs; and on the walls hung wide pasteboard charts, with unknown figures staring down black and fierce upon us. There were flower pots in the window, and one on the desk which stood at the end of the room before all the tables. Other women stood around with children by their sides, and the children stared curiously at one another as if unsure as to what was going to happen, and who would be friend or enemy when it did happen. I wanted to be told which one of the chairs was going to be mine. Then I could feel more as if I had a place here in this alien room.

The teacher of my first grade was an unmarried woman who had taught two generations of pupils before me. Her face was small and pointed, with wizened and wrinkled skin which gave her an ageless look. She was tall and thin, and her hands looked as if they were always cold. She had a way with children that put them at their ease, and perhaps that is why she was still teaching. We learned to read about Baby Ray and his animals, his dog and cat and cow and hen, and there were large colored pictures on every page which showed the little boy and his playmates. I came to feel as if Baby Ray were almost someone I had really known.

Naturally, the biggest influence on me that first year was the stimulus of being with so many children. After I came to know some of the little boys and girls in my room, it was all I could do to restrain myself from talking with them during the class times. And sometimes my restraint was not strong enough. The teacher would call my name, and I was embarrassed because I had done wrong. But there was so much I wanted to say and so much I wanted to find out from the others.

When I began to learn words, and could tell one by seeing it on paper anywhere, not just in the big print of the reader, it was a proud moment. I would go home and take the magazines Mother and Daddy read so easily and study through the sentences to pick out the three and two letter words I knew. Now I felt that I was beginning to find the key to a door which had been locked fast before. I could hardly wait to learn more words, and still more, so that I might read as well as they. I was learning to write too. There had been a few letters I could make before, the two-sided triangle of an A with the bar across the middle, the half-open circle of a C, the bars and straight line of an E. But this was different. This was combining all those letters into words, and saying to someone else a thing you had held in the little storeroom of your mind.

BEGINNING SCHOOL was more for me than a contact with new people. It was contact with new devices for play and entertainment. One of these was the slide. It seemed tremendous to me at the time, that slide with its tall tower of steep steps leading one by one to the top, and then the long, curved sweep to the ground. Climbing those steps the first few times, how miserable I felt. Other children were in front of me and other children behind, there was no turning back. I must go on, up, up, while the ground grew dizzier below me; then I must stand at that pinnacle and balance myself to sit down for the slide. Down, down, down, with the earth rushing up to meet me, and the ground stinging through my shoes against my feet, as I landed safe and sound.

The touch of the metal slide was immediate and pressing against our skin. On summer days, I remember it burned with the gathered heat of the sun, but there was at the same time an exquisite torture in the swift sting. In the winter, on raw windy days, how unmercifully cold that steel could be, as if the passage of a hundred warm little bodies over its surface would not warm it one iota.

Sometimes we slid down on our stomachs, slowing the swiftness of passage with our hands, clutched along the sides. Then, indeed, would it seem as if I were plunging to meet the ground, and in that brief moment all the colors of the green trees and brown dirt and blue sky would mingle in a kaleidoscope of moving color. Slowly, they came aright again and we clambered to our feet and off of the slide for the impatient one waiting at the top to have his turn.

Another of the playthings new to me was the catwalk. It was an iron affair standing some six or seven feet high with fifteen or twenty iron bars placed horizontally parallel to each other, with a pair of steps leading up at each end to the first bars. The idea was to swing by one's arms from the bars, progressing along the row by catching one bar after the other with first one hand, then the other. It was strenuous exercise, and for unpracticed muscles, almost impossible the first few times. Yet, how great a defeat to have to drop to the ground in the middle of the catwalk. Many's the time I hung on by sheer determination, with my arms feeling as if they would pull from their sockets, just to reach the end of the walk, and not be forced to drop in defeat. How dominant was the rule of competition, even in those first small years of school.

WALKING WAS one of the things my father did best. By this, I do not mean that his carriage was the perfect combination of a stage cross and a physical posture poster. I mean that when he walked there was vitality and meaning and purpose in every step he took. It was my father who first taught me that walking could be something more than simply a mode of transportation, a method of getting to and from. Oh, infinitely more. He illustrated for me the fact that finding one's feet on the earth is a joyous experience, that through physical contact with leaves and yellow-green fern fronds, grey rock, slushy spring mud, a person can learn the feel of nature in his bones.

"Reading is fine, little girl," he said once when he had found it difficult to bring me away from my book, "but it can't do what this can."

"This" was the hill behind our house, the stream behind the hill, and the mountain which rose sharp and like a backdrop behind them all. All my childhood seems to have been shadowed against these mountains.

"This is the reality," he said. "The books are only how someone else has seen these things. But you've got to go out and see them for yourself." It was true.

Our walks were usually in the evening, in that time of day between sundown and complete darkness which has been sentimentalized by so many poets. There was a routine attached to this walk. My father found his old felt hat, took down the long peeled walking stick, asked my mother and me if we were ready, and started slowly in the direction we were to take on our jaunt

Seven

that particular evening. By that time, our little dog, a Fox Terrier with an unclipped curling tail and too much pep for a several-times mother, had heard the preparations and knew the signals as well as we did. Running, circling, darting ahead, dashing back—with how much joy she could enter into our plans and go wild in the prospect of a walk together. So we would go through the woods, or beside the creek, or over a field, hearing those twittering comfortable sounds birds make when they have found their nest for the night—smelling the lushness of summer heat cooling on the leaves and bark in the darkening shadows—absorbing the relaxation that everything around us seemed to be enjoying.

This is one of the times I have missed most when I have lived in a city. This moment of hush. This moment of quiet expectancy. True, that when evening comes to the city in the summertime you find men in shirt sleeves reading the newspapers, women with tired faces fanning themselves as they sit along their doorsteps and talk with one another. But there is always the radio blaring behind them. There is always the street with its machine noises rattling in front of them. There is never any hush. There is simply never any moment when you feel—like I sometimes felt when I was a child in the country—as if now is the moment when some spirit is coming quite close, is perhaps speaking, is certainly communicating with you in some strange intangible manner you cannot explain and can only dimly realize.

Holes, too, played a major role in our excursions. They were exciting. Really interesting holes were rare. They were to be watched for and studied. When I was quite small I remember becoming aware of my father's stick pointing around a hole, heaping a few leaves before it, or simply remaining still, focusing on its object.

Thus, for a long while, he never overtly called my attention to these dozen various phenomena, nor did he speak to me about them. But I began to wonder. I even began to explore for myself, to watch for myself. What little lives filled those holes? Where did the entrance lead? I watched and hoped, but never could I see any of the occupants of these holes, either coming from or going to their abodes.

Then one day, quite unexpectedly, Daddy said, "What do you s'pose lives in it?" I looked up from where I was crouching beside our driveway. "I don't know," I said. "That's why I was watching." Then, on inspiration: "A snake?"

"No," my father said, in the short upturned way he had of saying no. "No, it's not a snake. Everyone always thinks holes are for snakes. He sees a hole and says, 'Oh, look, a snake hole.' That is, everyone who doesn't know. But there are lots of different kinds of holes. I guess this one is for a chipmunk."

Of course I knew what a chipmunk was. Mother called them ground squirrels. These were little furry animals a rich chestnut brown color with stripes down their soft mottled backs and a tail which gave away their relationship to the gray squirrel who could build in trees.

"I guess he came here for a reason," Daddy said. "When we built the driveway here we put in large stones as a bed and filled in on top of them with gravel. Well, I guess our little chipmunk has found lots of places among the stones for a roomy home."

I could see quite spacious rooms between two immense stones, where a tiny chipmunk might sleep most happily.

"Are all of the holes around chipmunk holes, Daddy?" I asked.

"Most of them I guess," he said.

"Then why are they so different? Some here near our house, some hidden away in the woods, some large and very round and some so little and ragged around the edges?"

"Well, why are our houses so different?"

From then on, I knew chipmunks, and all animals, in a way different from what I had ever known them before.

Sometimes on our walks we really had an objective, however. Some definite place we were headed, someone we were going to see. Often, this was a neighbor family living below us on the gravel road but before the highway. We three would go along the road slowly and steadily, passing another house or two, watching the creek which wound around close to the road, walking toward the companionship of other people. When we reached our destination we usually sat on the porch, Mother and Daddy talking with the other three adults—the man and his wife and their middle-aged daughter. She was a slim fastidious woman, their daughter, always cleaning something. Later she was to take the responsibility of her unwell mother, after her father died, and realize herself compelled to a duty she could not, because she would not, escape. But on those evenings, the conversation slipped by like threads through a shuttle, making only a background for the real pattern, the real colors. The porch was covered thick with kudzu vine. As we sat there in the security of familiar voices, the summer moon shone full and near through the great leaves, scattering strange shapes which for all the world were like the hieroglyphs of some ancient, unknown language. Now I would be listening to what the voices said, but then it was only the rhythm of what they spoke that reached me. Through the warm still air, the sprawling shadows spread by the kudzu vine and the maple tree stretched there before me. How distant was my world from theirs—how almost in another universe.

Then walking home later, hearing only the sounds of the disturbed gravel under our feet, the moon stretching shadows of ourselves before us, how alone we seemed in a vast silent world. Only we three moving in the circle of the dark mountains. How much a part of it all my father was; how warm and familiar my mother seemed; how glad I was for them there in the blazing moonlight.

CHILDREN ARE more straightforward in their curiosity about physical disabilities than are grown people. They gaze with direct look at any deformity and speak their thoughts for all to hear. There are none of the furtive glances or whispered allusions of tactful adults. The child's way is the kinder way I think.

At first, perhaps not so. But after a while the whispers and the nudges assume unwarranted proportions; the criticism and pitying take on the semblance of shadows, and who can cope with the intangibility of an image?

Children in the mountains are often deformed physically, or mentally and nervously impaired in some degree. Perhaps the proportion seems more than in certain other sections because the opportunity and desire for operations in such cases is less than in other sections. Much of it is due to frequent intermarriages. However, this as a direct cause is becoming less and less in the mountain sections I know; at one time intermarriage was almost without alternative if a family lived in an isolated section. Rapid succession of children, diseases in the parents, lack of proper nourishment both before and after birth: all these are causes, too, for the incapacitation of their children. I saw families of seven or eight, the children all small and no more than a year or a year and a half apart, and I can remember being repulsed and being held by the gaunt unhealthiness of their faces. Small "young'uns" with teeth already decayed and decaying, their hair straggling in thin wisps down their heads, and in the springtime, a mass of sores on their legs and arms. These were called "spring sores," and were raw, bloody splotches of infected skin and flesh. To my father, from another section, they were inconceivable, but my mother had seen them before. They were accepted as inevitable by the children and mountain people themselves. Spring was a blossoming time, a time of light quick winds and teeming earth, of returning birds and returning warmth; it was, as well, a time of sores, of patent medicine, and tonics. Nothing came beautiful and free alone; there was some element of worry, of sickness, death, or ruined crops, in every season and every day. The babies grew into childhood with this burden of unhappiness and responsibility heavy around them. Their childhood was soon over, and their maturity was something untimely and without richness. It was, it is, a pitiful thing to see.

This is naturally not true in all cases, as no one broad fact is ever applicable to every family and every community. But I have seen it so more than once, many dozen times more than once, and it is something not to be forgotten. Rather, to be considered.

One of the first mountain children I ever knew was a little girl who lived in the last house on the road which ran in front of where I lived. It was steep on the side of the mountain and very poor. I saw her one day going along the road in front of my house, carrying a can of kerosene oil which she had bought at the little store some three miles farther down the pavement. I wanted to know anyone near my age, and so I talked with her. The next day she came to see me. Her arms were thin and pinched, there was something ill about her whole physical frame. I, too, was thin and wiry because I was always active, but hers was a different sort of leanness. It was the leanness of lack of food and too much work, not the natural leanness of youth.

She stayed through the morning, and when we were ready to eat lunch, my father and mother asked her to eat with us. She sat at the end of the breakfast room table, her shoulders rounded over her plate. I remember the hard wrinkled flesh on her hands and arms; it was like a woman's hardness. She could have been no more than ten or eleven. My father served her plate and suddenly she did a memorable thing. She hunched forward and with bony clutching fingers she grabbed at the pieces of meat among the vegetables before her. Quickly, fearfully, as if afraid someone might grab it from her, she stuffed the meat into her mouth. Her dark brown eyes were large and tense above her mouth.

"I love meat," she said. The words lay on the air with pregnant heaviness.

There was something about the way she spoke that made them fierce as hate, persistent as love. We did not speak or eat, but watched her tear the bits of lamb into pieces with her fingers and push them into her mouth. Something elemental had come into our lives with a vivid streak and had lighted up the whole horizon. We found no answer to make.

Seven

eight

MY TEACHER IN THE second grade was
a small, thin-haired woman who always
smelled faintly of cold cream. Her hands
were hard and slender; in fact, there
was nothing soft or pliable about her. She was a good teacher.
Yet there was something about her which remained aloof and
serious above the contacts with us, and of all the teachers in
my grammar school I remember her with more formality and
distance. There were no emotional ties between herself and us
children; she taught us spelling and arithmetic and reading, and
at the end of the afternoon period, when three o'clock came,
we closed our books and that was that. Yet at the same time, I
remember her with more real regret and sadness than any of the
other teachers. She was so much a type, such a product of what
the community had thought a school teacher should be, especially an unmarried lady school teacher, that she fitted into our
school days and we forgot her. They had made her into this little
conventional mold as surely as if they had set out and planned
what her life should be.

I sometimes wonder now if she *was* happy. What she did after
she left school and went home, what she thought of as she ate
her breakfasts and dinners, and fixed her lunch each morning in
a neat brown paper bag. Once after I had left her grade and had
gone up a step or two, I saw her downtown. She was standing
on a street corner waiting for the bus. The dark blue pin-striped
suit was brushed as neat as a pin, and her hat was of the plainest

sort. In her hand she held two or three small packages, mostly from the five and dime store, as I could tell by the paper. There was something startling and a little disconcerting in seeing her standing there so straight and prim and lonely. She did not see me, and I felt like it was almost disrespectful and unkind to watch her when she was not expecting to be watched. Perhaps I felt a little like children must suppose God to feel, as he looks down on them and sees their most unconscious moments, even when they least expect it. So she stood, and I knew that if I had passed a bit closer to her I would have breathed the vague odor of cold cream. After a few minutes the bus came, and quietly, unobtrusively, she took her place in the line. I saw the girl behind her, in a bright flowered dress and red jacket, look her over quickly, thoroughly and give a little shrug of disdain, as she climbed up the steps behind her. Then the bus drove off.

THE FOODS one eats as a child are forever engraved upon his memory. I, for one, do not believe now that the "pies mother used to make" are any better, if people only knew it, than any of the pies they eat later. It is simply that during childhood their tastes are uncultivated, their energies more abundant, food is more welcome and therefore tastes as it will never taste again.

I remember my Aunt Maude's biscuits, my grandmother's cornbread, and my mother's yeast bread. Why all these foods I recall best are in the bread category, I do not know. But there they were.

When I was small, my mother did not permit me to eat biscuits. We seldom had hot breads at home as was the usual Southern custom, because my father liked the "light bread." My Aunt Maude, however, felt that I was too thin, too birdlike, and so she often stuffed me with hot biscuits when I went up the creek to visit her. They were delicious morsels, hot and crumbly, and the odor from them was incomparable. She cut huge slices of fresh butter and slid them between each biscuit so that the butter might melt with fragrant richness into the flaky dough.

Eight

"These biscuits won't hurt her and they make her get some fat on those little legs," Aunt Maude used to say, as she slipped them off the hot pan, one by one, and thrust them into my hand. They didn't make me fat, but they did hurt me in one respect. As the old mountaineers say, they hurt me for want of more like them.

My grandmother's cornbread came a little later, after the biscuit supply had moved, along with my aunt, to another part of the state. She served the cornbread with her vegetable dinners, and it flavored all it touched. I don't know how she mixed the simple formula of meal and buttermilk and soda, but it combined the odor and flavor of all the nuts I ever ate. It broke apart in your hand and the steam rose up around your face. The best part was the crust, which sometimes stuck to the black iron skillet. Then it was a race to see who could get the gold-brown pieces first. I usually won because I was the only child around the stove, and had only my own interests to tend to.

Mother seldom made the bread she used, at least it seemed seldom to me, but what an occasion when she did. The process required a whole day, for the dough had to rise twice, and called for kneading in between. The baking phase was what I enjoyed most, although there was no little amount of curiosity attached to the rising. Mother would roll and knead the dough, then place long strips into a pan far too large, it seemed to me. But when the dough began to rise, how the proportions of the pan shrank. The bread puffed slowly, expanding with the slow heat of our wood-range warmer, compelled by some strong force.

"What makes it rise?" I naturally wanted to know.

"Something I put in it that I buy at the market," Mother said. "It's called yeast."

"What is yeast?" I wanted to know more definitely.

"This yeast I get comes in a square little cake," she said. "Really yeast is a plant, I guess. It's so small you couldn't even see it if you tried. But look how it works in my bread. Hundreds of little germs they are, in there working for us."

And that was one of my first lessons in biology.

When the bread was baking, it was a joy to wait for it to turn darker and darker on the top until finally the loaf was finished and its crust was the color of grained oak wood. We could hardly wait to taste it.

MY FATHER was very fond of bread and milk. I can remember him making many a meal off of a pitcher of cold milk and a half dozen slices of bread, preferring it to other food on the table. It was his favorite dish for supper—we ate our main meal in the middle of the day until I started to school and mother thought I should have hot food at night—and I can see him sitting in the green half-light of summer evening, slowly breaking the slices into his bowl, then pouring the yellow milk carefully over the pieces.

There was something about the loving way he performed this simple task that transformed it into a ritual. It was compelling. It made the combination seem the best cuisine concoction that was possible. I always ate bread and milk when he did, for I could not resist the temptation to enjoy such manifold pleasure.

Bread and milk portray certain facts about my father. It is an illustration of the simplicity he sought in everything—not only sought but enjoyed. The simplest dress, the least affected manners, the plainest people—these were all that he was part of. Living in nature as he had, being of a philosophical turn of mind as he was, it was the wisdom of his years that he knew it was not the ornamental or the extravagant that was basic and enduring. It was the plant subjected to the weather that withstood the wind; it was the heifer of sturdy pedigree and no ostentatious show of butter-fat that withstood the dangers of milk-fever at the birth of her calf; it was the unsophisticated mind, unconcerned with fashion, uncluttered with ambition, that withstood the doubt inherent in the paradoxes of certainty and found in life one truth, or maybe two, that it could feel was valid.

Such was the quality of my father's mind. The texture of its fibre was sinewy and strong as locust roots, unlike the pithy fibre of so many complex minds I have later found, which, when the surface was peeled away, lay like an open reed by the river, with the core drawn easily out and only a deceiving shell left as remainder.

It is not often today a child grows up in the presence of a person wise with age, so inclined toward the philosophical. I felt the singularity of my home-life early. I saw that there were no families around us who read or walked together regularly as we did; that there was almost no one who went out as seldom as we did; and that certainly there was no father about who quoted Scott and Tennyson as easily as the daily paper, nor any mother who preferred raking leaves and polishing her aluminum to joining an afternoon club. For a while, I think the differences puzzled me. Then I came to see that we were happy in things these other people disregarded. Our goals were different. We wanted peace and thoughtfulness. They wanted excitement. Each had its way of life.

I gradually came to discover that it was only in this atmosphere, which my father and mother had created in our house and which was inherent in the woods, that I could actually feel or think. At school, in town, at other's homes, I had sensations, I gathered impressions. But all these impressions and sensations were disconnected and jumbled until I could get home and there reassemble them all in my mind and coordinate them in my feelings and my thoughts until they had meaning.

During free hours at school I could never write my papers or think through my arithmetic problems as clearly as I could at home. Some may say this was merely an overdeveloped attachment to a place or person, or that it was a matter of association. Perhaps so, but what is attachment or association if it is not also atmosphere. And it was that atmosphere, or "sense" of the place, I can say, that made me at home in one locality and out of joint in the other. Perhaps I could merely say that at home and in nature I was drawn out of myself into something larger. In the presence of the excitement and confusion which characterized other people and places, the shallower, more intensely personal side of life was brought into play, nay even into competition. Since this was neither the world I had been accustomed to, nor the part of myself I had cultivated, I found it unimaginative and uninteresting. Exciting, yes, but somehow not altogether to be trusted.

I believe my father was Puritanical in many ways. There was a sternness of character in him, a toughness of fibre, that did not yield itself readily to alien ideas, or even change. He spoke for himself once when he said to me,

"Don't let this business of being 'broad-minded' keep you from being strong-minded. You know, little girl, a person can have so many views he doesn't know what he really believes about anything. Figure it out for yourself. That's all I want. Be foxy about new fads—or old ones for that matter. Just because a thing's old or new doesn't make it right. Use your own mind and maybe you'll be able to pick what's true."

He was what many today would label conservative, I suppose. (There are so many labels one begins to feel almost manufactured.) But one quality he did have which redeemed him forever with all his solitary ruggedness from being an Epictetus, an early Salem Puritan. That quality was a sense of humor. It was not the rich, droll humor like my mother knew; rather, it was a humor which saw the ironies in life, the paradoxes in men, and fitted them together in a philosophy of life which found these facts a human healthy part of natural life. For is not nature herself, in all her realms, filled with these qualities of paradox and irony? Realizing this, my father must view life with humor for himself and his own rigid beliefs, knowing everything was subject to change, as well as humor for others. Often when he was most touched with sympathy for someone, or riled to anger against someone for what he believed was their own stupidity, I have seen him pause while a quick look of humor and laughter passed over his face at the thought of some incongruity in the whole trifling affair.

It has made me wonder, since I have grown older, if God—or our creator, whatever you choose to call him—does not have a great sense of humor, and if sometimes he does not pause for gargantuan laughter at an animal so perfect and so foolish as man, who can make himself wings, to feel the freedom of space, and in the end use those wings for the mass death of his own kind.

I wonder if a man has ever lived who realized the confusions and paradoxes struggling in another man's life. I wonder if any person has ever understood any other person with all the tolerance he deserved.

Once Daddy said to me, "One thing I want you to remember, little girl, and it is this: blame no one, praise no one, accuse no one. Everyone lives his life in his own way, and you will live yours. Don't interfere with his life, or try to judge it. Stand on your own feet."

Certainly this was what he did. I cannot remember him ever interfering in the slightest way with anyone else's affairs; yet he was sure to help any physical distress or need.

For himself, he had accepted loneliness long before, had perhaps welcomed it. I remember him saying to my mother, "I've never been lonely in my life. I've never had what's called 'the blues' either. Even when my first wife was so sick, and after she died, I did not feel lonely. Sad, yes, but I had always known that we are alone in this life, so I could not feel lonely."

It was difficult for my mother to understand this, for she was the believer in humanity, if my father was the believer in nature. She had tasted loneliness. One is born with loneliness in the mountains; its cry is ever-present. When the adult realization of every man's innate aloneness comes, it is not so overwhelming if you have lived in the mountains, for something in your spirit, since childhood, has whispered this was so. The unfelt wind howling behind the hills, the starkness of November rains, the call of nightbirds through the silence, all are testaments to the final realization of loneliness.

So my mother had been always aware of the fact, but she had been also dependent on people. There was something in her nature which made her want to help people, want to do for them, and although she knew that she could not count on them in the last test, perhaps, she nonetheless wanted to know them now. Both of them could be happy without other people, but when someone did call upon us, I always felt that it was my mother who was most glad to see them. In conversation, when such people came, it was always Mother who took the lead, of necessity. Daddy did not suit his moods or levels of idea and thought to suit our visitors. He remained inviolate, himself always. Those who would, might come to him—and they would find him a rich storehouse. For the others, they might chatter on as they liked but he would not disrobe his mind and descend to them. He felt no need for self-assertion, which need is back of so much conversation. There was no need for him to inflate his ego before others because he had already placed the needs of his ego outside the realm of men, in the realm of nature. And in nature, the ego of a single person is swallowed up in the mystery of the whole, in the vastness of which it is a part. With such an attitude, he was not humiliated or made small in any way, but simply drawn together and lifted above the smaller, passing assertions of self.

I was aware of these subtleties, as we sat with visitors in our familiar living room when I was a child, and it was probably because I did not know as many people as some children do when they are small, and therefore I became more sharply aware of them when they were in a group. I caught many of the subtleties between people, and in their character. People came to be magic for me, they were the strange element in my life—not the things of nature which are strange to many children. The consciousness of these responses between people ran like quicksilver through my perception and I became a sort of mirror, as most children are, reflecting the things about me.

Eight

WHAT IS THE STRANGE miraculous force which works through all the seasons, bringing to life, nourishing, putting to rest, the inhabitants of an entire world of plants? It is a force to be sung for other reasons than its producing of beauties. Indeed, the beauty, once we know its functions, was not created for the mere sake of prettiness alone, but as the fulfillment of a cause and a design. How egotistical we humans are to believe, as we do, that flowers were placed on earth for our enjoyment, their colors chosen for our pleasure. But how much more dignity and reason to the whole purpose of living, when we know that plant life is the base and foundation for all life, that without that magic substance called chlorophyll which manufactures, through sunlight and by the combination of water and carbon dioxide, the all-important sugar, there would be no organic life upon this earth. Consider then the work of the plant adornments, the blossoms themselves, which is to aid in the process of reproduction. How filled with wonder this natural world is!

Whatever that force may be behind the rising and falling of sap, the blooming and withering of flowers, the miracle exists. That was the fact I cherished and held to. For the world of plants and blooming things was real and close to me. My mother particularly had passed on to me this passion, in the very genes which formed me, and through all her following example. Flowers were the turning of the seasons, the comings and the goings of time. From the crisp whiteness of spring to the lush golden fall, they bloomed and withered, ate, grew, drank, reproduced, and through it all I was allowed to watch their cycle of life.

The earliest flower I ever found in the springtime I discovered one afternoon in late winter. Spring had hardly suggested its presence, and it was beyond my hopes to find any sign of its nearness. I merely walked in the raw windy afternoon because a mood was upon me and I wished to be alone. The desire to be alone is strange in a child, and yet I often wanted to be without people. Perhaps because I never felt alone when there was any living object around me.

The ground was wet with recent rain and winter thaw, so I looked for a stone to sit on. Under the shelter of a great, grey lichen-covered rock I saw some green leaves growing. I pulled away the piles of drifted oak and chestnut and poplar leaves, and there bloomed a trailing arbutus. It was the first throb of fertility in a ground long dormant. The pastel flowers poked their petals out between the green, brown-edged arbutus leaves and gave the signal that spring was closer at hand than we had suspected. I raked back more of the leaves, leaving enough however for the plant to feel some of the accustomed protection the rich, rotting mass had given it. The arbutus flower looked so fragile and unprepossessing under the looming massiveness of the grey rock. For all its smallness it seemed to say, "I grow here in spite of what you could do. You are only a stone, but I am green and living."

Always in spring there was the spicewood. It often came in March, sometimes during April, and the tender yellow and green of its flowers and foliage was a sight to make me leap as I walked. They were tiny flowers, close to the branch of the tree, and they were yellow the color of fresh-churned butter, pale and moist. In the springtime, they were more excellent than many a gaudier flower which bloomed in the summer but came when our taste was satiated.

Sometimes I would break twigs from the spicewood tree or bush and brew some spicewood tea. I had heard the mountain people tell of it, and I must try it for myself. It was a light amber color and tasted to suit its name, faintly of spices, with a wild tang. I made three cups, one for each of us. It was not unlike another tea I made, out of sassafras roots. What a time I had digging for those roots! But the tea was good, and I had been careful to get no more of the root than would not injure the bush. Incidentally, the berry of this sassafras was a perfect exhibit in color. It was a deep blue-black over the entire surface except for one end which was a pure cadmium yellow. The end of the berry which was thus colored fit into a thick scarlet calyx, the calyx

Eight

....

being held by a matching red stem. The blue-black, scarlet, and cadmium yellow. No wonder birds were attracted to the sassafras berries for food.

After the spicewood comes a sweep of flowers which lasts throughout the summer, wilting only with the coming of autumn. There is the pussy willow with its greyish-blue fur which gave it its name. An old pussy willow stood at an end of my Aunt Maude's porch across the brook from our house, and the ripening of the grey buds was a thing to watch. As they grew older, the grey turned to a dusty yellow from small fuzzy hairs which grew on the buds. They looked like the delicate whiskers on an old sedate tabby.

At the base of the hill which rose immediately back of our house, there was a moist leaf-filled depression. In this slight depression each spring a minor miracle took place. It was the uncurling of the ferns. We watched the process day by day and marveled at it. First appeared the yellow-green sprout so tender it was almost white. Then slowly and steadily the little sprout would force its way through the leaves surrounding it until it stood many inches above the ground, still curled tight in its immaturity. This process of the unwinding was what we most enjoyed. It was to watch this young brittle frond grow strong and green, to watch it unfurl as a snail might uncurl his shell if he could. There behind our house for the whole summer grew a bed of these ferns, tall and wide. Everyone who saw them remarked on their size and healthy dark green color. But only we who had seen them begin in the coolness of spring and rise indomitably toward the sunshine and air could experience the thrill of how the ferns had grown.

Last that I will mention, perhaps most beautiful, were the dogwoods and violets. Along the hills, far and wide, the creamy four-petaled blossom of the dogwood flowered to life. It was a poor man's magnolia and one could not help but notice it. But the violets had to be sought for. I was lucky, for year after year they grew in the ravine between the hill and the mountain

Eight

86

behind my house. It was a poor hill where they grew, but they must have found what nourishment they needed, for their color was as deep a purple as I have ever seen and they grew thick and plentiful. It made me throb with happiness to see that patch of violets growing there and walk among them. I picked them by the handfuls, to float in a glass dish filled with cold spring water at home, but even with the ones I took, there never seemed to be any missing.

There was also a stream in that ravine, an overflow from our spring reservoir which stood above. In the soggy swamp-like places where the little stream did not flow well, there grew another type of violet. It was white and very tall. The leaves were decidedly heart-shaped and grew high beside the violet. To trace with one's finger down the side of the violet stem, down into the cold dark water, was a good feeling. They grew there within sight of one another, those two violets, one short and near the ground on a sun-hot hill, the other tall and white in the moist marsh. Strange differences inherent in seed and in environment.

Summer flowers—who could name the dozens which grew by the roadside, out in the meadows and fields and in the woods. The shiny yellow buttercup in almost any grassy place, so pretty to the stranger, such a bane to any farmer. Or the cardinal flower, beside a stream, or the Indian paintbrush in the woods, both red with a clear unmixed purity. The wild iris, called flags by some, light blue with its purple and yellow adornments. Or who could deny the summer weeds their beauty? The velvet-leafed mullein growing in old fields with a yellow stocky flower tapering to a point; the plant used to make a mullein tea that the mountain people drank. And the ragweed, green and dusted heavily with yellow pollen. Most common of all perhaps, the Queen Anne's Lace. I remember it growing in quantities along the stone road which ran by our house to the paved highway. It stood tall—two or three feet sometimes—looking so much like a piece of lace with its broad white surface made of hundreds of tiny blossoms and with one single drop of dark maroon in its center, that I often

Eight

made chains out of the flowers and pretended they were veils or trailing skirts of an exquisite lace dress. Feeling part of nature as I did, I could not always resist human temptation to think of it as something created as a supplement to myself. Underneath, however, I think I always knew it was a life whole in itself, being neither supplement nor servant.

When the purple ironweeds and the goldenrods bloomed along the dusty hills, or roads, autumn had surely come. There was no turning back. The trees shouted with color now as well as the late flowers, and the sumac blazed red in the edges of fields. Its stalky red flower would remain red throughout the winter. The poke weed, too, had produced its purple, strong-odored berries, and although we had dug the tender sprouts of the weed in the early spring and eaten them boiled and flavored with bacon, we were now warned that it was a dangerously poison food. It seemed uncanny to me, like holding a bottle of medicine which had helped you before and turning it to a different side and seeing there suddenly the cross bones and skull. Fickle plant to about-face so easily. As to the berries, another girl and myself tried a stunt we had heard and squeezed a panful through an old sieve in an attempt to make some ink. The juice was a reddish-purple and looked pretty, though splotchy, against the white writing paper. It soon turned to a brown color, however, as the weed it had come from turned brown in the winter, and after a while the ink faded away altogether.

Now the winter had come, bringing into their own display the lichens and mosses, the red and green galax leaves in clusters along the hill, and at Christmas time the white berried mistletoe, hanging high off the ground in its parasitic growth along some tree branch. Its berries were like seed pearls with the dark brittle leaves as a green background. The pines, the laurels, the rhododendrons showed green everlasting along the barren mountainsides.

IN THE SPRING, there was the excitement of setting hens and watching the chickens hatch. Mother usually began to set the hens sometime in March, and then at intervals through April she might set others so that we would have friers all during the summer. Sometimes we bought little chickens at the stores, and sometimes we set the eggs themselves. Either way was good.

At the seedstores, where we bought our chicks, there would be boxes piled on top of boxes, all filled with a cheeping, moving mass of yellow and grey and black and colors ranging in between. I liked to stand before these boxes, with only the thin wire between the chickens and myself, and watch the little things drink and peck at each other and at the floor. Sometimes one just stood at the side and cried, his voice shrill and continuous above the noises of the others. There seemed so many different kinds of chickens. White Rock, Bard Rock, Plymouth Rock, Leghorn, Rhode Island Red, Minorca, and on and on. How could anyone choose between them, and what were the differences? Then when Mother had bought her chickens, and the man had put them in a pasteboard box with holes punched in the sides, we took them home. How they peeped when we put them in the car! But after a while they would quiet down, and I would take the lid off and look at them, hardly able to keep my hands off of them, they were so fluffy and helpless. There they would be, crowded into one corner, pushing against each other, feeling security in their numbers and in their closeness to one another. They were like people I had seen, who seemed afraid to be alone, but somehow felt safe in a crowd.

Of course there was always the fear that a hen might not take the chickens. We would wait until after dark and then go out to the nest where the hen had decided to set. Mother would take the little chickens out of the box, while I held the box for her, and ever so gently she would push them under the wing of the unsuspecting hen. The flashlight would throw a small oval of light along the wall, and beyond the circle of light the hens and rooster on the perches would make quiet disturbed noises, moving uneasily on the long poles. The sounds were drowsy and feathery and blended with the odor of warm feathers and fresh straw in the nests. When the last chick was deposited, we could close the loose lid over the nest and throw the flashlight around the room. The hens would raise their heads and blink in the sudden brightness. Then we would go out, and the air smelled fresh and cool around us. I always hoped frantically that the hen would take her adopted chickens.

Once in a while Mother would go out the next morning, however, and find one of the little things picked to death, or find one bleeding and confused where the old hen had pecked it. When that happened, there was nothing to do but take the chickens away. If there was another hen setting we could put them under her, but if not, then we must take them in the house, if the weather was cold, and watch them until they were several days older and could care for themselves more capably. Mother did not like to have the chickens inside, even in the basement, but I loved it. I put fresh water before them constantly, and fed them oatmeal whenever I thought they could possibly eat it. It was nice to hear them cheeping together in little squeaks which sounded like chicken conversation when I came downstairs in the morning and put them near the basement window where they could get the sun. There was something warm and friendly about their small sounds, their contentment.

When we set the hen and hatched our own chickens, there was always the wait until they broke through the shells, and it seemed months long. Then one day Mother would say, "Come out to the chicken house," and there would be the eggs firm and hard, but with almost inaudible sounds coming through the shells of some. To look at the eggs it always seemed hard to believe that the chickens could live and grow and finally come out of this shell with all the equipment they would need to live their chicken life. I had thought eggs were put into the world for the purpose of providing us with material for cakes, and an occasional poached or scrambled egg for breakfast. Now I found they were for a purpose, but one quite different from what

Eight

....

90

I had supposed. Again, my little human ego was pricked with the pin of truth.

We would listen to the faint pecks on the shell, and then suddenly there would be a hole in the shell which grew gradually larger and larger. Sometimes Mother would help the struggling chick along, and peel off bits of the shell herself. There would be the chicken, new and wet, emerged for the first time into this large world of the chicken house. He was ugly and repulsive, looking so naked and wet, yet strangely interesting too. There was something helpless and other-worldish about him; the curious mystery of the beginning of any thing alive.

Sometimes there would be the squall of a hen at night, and we would know that some animal had found a way into the chicken house. How lonely a sound it was, breaking through the stillness, coming and going in one short burst of fear and helplessness. Then my father would crawl out of bed and find his slippers, take one of his heaviest canes and go out in the darkness. Usually it was a possum that had gotten into the chickens, and maybe he would still be sitting in a corner, his eyes bright and fierce in his pointed face, with the frightened hens hovered in the opposite corner of the house. Twice my father killed a possum in the night, and it was a memorable thing. Dead the animal looked so harmless. It seemed a shame to kill something so wild and free, yet we must keep our chickens, and he had been a marauder. So it went.

The worst loss was one night early in the summer, when we had fastened twenty-five young chickens in their coop and failed to inspect the edges to make sure there was not a single hole for animals to find. The next morning Mother opened the coop, but there was no rush of wings, no escape out into the morning as there usually was. One poor little fellow came hobbling out alone, crippled in the leg. Mother lifted the coop from the ground. There lay twenty-four dead chickens. They made a square pattern where the coop had surrounded them. She picked one up. Its neck was pierced. "A weasel," she said, her

Eight

face grim and flushed, and laid it down again. We felt a great sense of loss, for they had been fine chickens and we had only weaned them from the hen a few days before.

So it was that we came to know all sides of nature: the peaceful beauty, and the constant battle. All about us it went on. Between the hawks and all the smaller birds; between the owls and all the running mice and ground squirrels; between the foxes and the baying dogs. And when the battle came into our backyard and in our woods, we must protect our own and kill what we must kill. It was strange to me that no life could seem to exist without the death of some other life.

nine

....

WHEN I WAS IN THE third grade, my teacher was particularly interested in our imaginations. She either wanted to awaken them or she wanted to develop them; I do not recall which was her purpose. I do know it would have been better if she had left the matter entirely alone. She was always calling for us to "see things in our mind's eye." She would put a picture on the wall before us and then remove it, or she would set a vase of flowers in the window and then suddenly take it away.

"Now see if you can remember it, *in your mind's eye*," she would say, with a tone that made it seem as if the task would be a difficult one for us.

Then we closed our eyes, each of us, and reported as to our visions. I was always confused by these tests, or trials, or whatever they might be called. Once I had my eyes tightly closed, a series of colors and shapes began to dance across the darkness before me. Such shapes and colors as they were, triangles, squares, and figures of many sides. Colors were shapeless and became presences in themselves; yellow, greens, and violets all converging in veritable jigs of color. All at once I would be brought out of my carnival of sensations by the voice of the teacher.

"Can you all see the picture (or the flower)? Can you see the colors and the shapes?"

....

Then I could remember the object she was speaking of, but I was never sure of the "mind's eye" part. I thought perhaps a vision of the sought-after piece would come before my eyes, like a picture in a photograph book, and that I would see inch by inch the living thing before me. That it appeared in my memory, and that I could recall its form, made no impression upon me. And this was the worst part of such teaching. It stressed the photographic reproduction of an object, not the imagined and adorned. I thought that all our teacher sought after was a likeness, which was true, and that any significance or interpretation I might bring to bear on the matter was due to fault on the part of my mind's eye. It was the difference between the photographer and the painter. The former takes the object as it is and can never change or alter it from its actuality—even remembering the wonders which his angle-shots and filters may achieve; but the painter paints a part of himself into the reproduction which he makes; he brings his hand and eye and spirit to the task.

So it was only when I began to grow aware of an imagination as such, that I began to lose my way toward finding it again. For an imagination was something I had possessed, is something which all children possess, and it had interpreted the world for me, and made the things about me as rich in possibilities as the dreams of any far away land. Imagination had known no bounds and held no scorns. Nothing was too small that it might not be seized upon and translated into a thing of wonder, of great meaning, of beauty, or simply of whetted interest. A leaf blown on the ground and rolling along the road with an autumn wind beneath it, a spool from which the thread has all been taken, a box which once held the breakfast oatmeal, a soggy place in the woods where one may dig a little with a stick and find then and there the bursting forth of an unknown spring: these are the things which act as springboards from which imagination can fly into unheard of realms. Nothing big or pretentious here; only the smallest things seen every day.

For that is one mistake we make when we are grown. We demand size so often, in place of the other elements we really need. Is it thick, how many pages does it have, we ask of the latest book; how large is it we ask about a friend's new house. How many acres does he have we ask about an acquaintance who buys a farm. Instead, and what a child would want to know, the questions really are: what is the quality of the book; what can it bring to me or I to it? Or, is the house livable? Is it a home? Or, what sort of a farm did he buy? And were the acres, or maybe just the acre, wooded land or pasture? Were there streams or hills or trees? Because those are the elements that make all the difference. The difference between days lived richly and completely, invoking all the attributes of mind and heart and spirit; or days lived on the margin of existence, on the thin edge of reality, always on the borderline of something entire and satisfying.

If I lost the greatest part of that imagination which was once mine, and which served as the wide swinging door to a hundred different paths down which I could go figuratively, and never actually, running, skipping, dancing, at least there was one thing which I never lost. One thing which is true of childhood, but which held over for me, and has continued through until today. That was an inability to become bored. I had no talent for a dozen new toys when I was little, I had no talent for boredom. I have none now. For this, I am glad.

I suppose if the imaginations of grown people were as fertile as the imaginations of children, our hunger for ownership would be in part dismayed. For it does not take ownership to satisfy the mind, or please the senses. And the fancy needs only the sight or the smell or the touch of its object before it goes winging away into a world of its own. Moreover, the spirit surrounded and closed in by too many things demanding ownership and responsibility is confused by a flood of sensation, a downpour of stimulation. This is why a child not surrounded each Christmas and holiday by dozens of playthings and amusements from his uncles and aunts and parents and friends is more simple

Nine

....

95

and less satiated than a child who has this inappropriate display. The latter's fancy is dulled, at least is stunted, because his fancy is bewildered and his time too filled with these mechanical things around him. What chance has he to create stories, when all around him are books filled with stories and pictures he has not seen or heard? What chance has he to build a tower from a carefully collected pile of handworn spools, when in the closet are building sets which hold the blocks of every size and shape to fit into exact building miniatures? What reason has he to sit on a sun-warmed rock by the running creek and wait and hope with trembling heart for the sight of a darting lizard, when on the window sill of his room sits a perfect bowl with goldfish swimming clean and visible inside? No, it is not necessary to our imaginations that we own a mass of accumulated objects; it is possibly even better that we do not own them.

Then clearly, simply, our minds belong to ourselves and to the worlds they choose to create. And lacking fantastic abundances, we shall not be satiated. Lacking satiation there will be no boredom. It is not the appetite for things which "grows by what it feeds on." It is the appetite for imaginative living. And it grows into a life which welcomes all experiences, simplifies all mouthed obscurities, and makes death the greatest flint-rock of them all, the flint-rock which strikes the sharpest and the brightest fire.

WHEN I WAS nine years old I developed a habit of sending off for samples. Perhaps it is a stage most children go through, at least I have known several other sample-senders in children, and even a few adults. But with me, it became developed into a fine art. I think my habit must have come into existence when manufacturers of various products had reached the zenith of advertising through samples, for there was hardly a magazine which came to our house that did not contain a half dozen or so coupons inside which were to be clipped "along the dotted line." And we subscribed to a good many magazines.

At first I sent my coupons off in a letter, but then I found a way which would make the overhead much lighter. I wrote on a postal card. In the course of time I collected quite an assortment of articles, everything from lotion and bathsalts down to a new cereal just coming on the market. With all this array, I decided I should start a private store for myself, and I did. On the floor above my father's workshop I made myself a little counter, and Daddy, who found out what I was doing, made for me a whole system of shelves which resembled those in a real store. For days I collected paper bags and string, set my goods up for display, and finally went around to invite the people I knew: my mother, my grandmother and aunt, the woman who lived in the next house, and for variety and volume, one of the mountain families who lived above us, to come to the opening of my store.

They all came, the woman from up on the mountain bringing her little girl with her. They were not a mentally bright family, in fact they must have rated very low on the intelligence scale, and their very appearance indicated their dullness and ignorance. They stared with great brown eyes at everything that took place around them, and their mouths were constantly half open, perhaps from adenoids which should have been long since removed. "Now looky here, you be purty," the woman was constantly admonishing her little girl, with a jerk at her arm or hair.

I was disgusted that I had asked them now, for the woman who had moved into the house below us kept looking at them with disdainful surprise, and I could feel the prestige of my effort being diminished. Then, too, I realized that they would not be able to buy anything from my store; altogether it was too bad that I had asked them. And so I paid them little attention during the program I had planned, with my two small cousins as performers. Later, when I enumerated all my wares and sold some of them to my customers for a few pennies, I forgot all about the mountain woman. She sat, with her little girl, in a chair at the side, and watched what went on.

Nine

....

The others left, my mother asking them over on the porch to tea. I could hear them laughing about my "little store" as they left. Then suddenly the woman came forward. She startled me, for I had almost forgotten about her. She reached into the torn pocket at one side of her long coat and brought out a faded thread-bare purse. "I want two of those," she said, and pointed toward the bits of soap bars on the shelves. She fumbled in her purse, intent on the occasion, and laid a dime on the counter. I put the soap in a second-hand paper bag and handed it to her. I picked up the dime. I wanted it and yet, somehow, I did not want it. She had turned and was taking the child by the hand to go. A coat was too warm for a day like this; suddenly, I knew why she had worn it. Suddenly I saw the whole picture. The two little bars of soap—she could have gotten twice as much at any store. The dime was between us, meaning more to her than to me, for all the sizable proportions a dime had in my nine year eyes. And yet I did not move. She reached the steps and started down. I heard the door below into my father's workshop open, and then my mother's voice spoke. "Oh," she said to the woman, "here you are. I was just coming back to be sure you stopped in for some tea with the rest of us." Then the two of them went out together and I heard the door close behind them. A wave of gratitude went out to my mother. Perhaps she could atone for some of the guilty feeling that was inside of me. The pleasurable taste of the afternoon had gone for me, and the thrill of my selling, that was gone too. It was not such fun as I had thought to get something for nothing. Because somebody, somewhere, paid a price.

I DO NOT KNOW where the idea had its origination and beginning. I do not know where the idea finally vanished. But I do know that it came, and that it went, and that in between the coming and the going was an untold secret story.

I awoke one morning in spring, and I had decided to run away. There was no particular reason why I should leave home.

I was neither beaten nor locked into spidery towers, as children in fairy tales had been. There was no logical place where I could go and not be found. And yet the desire was there, as strong as any wish I ever knew, and just as real.

We owned an old tan leather suitcase which was somewhat smaller than the usual bag, and this I confiscated for my proposed journey. I spent one whole day gloating over it, finding it and carrying it out from its storage place and hiding it in some place thought safe enough. Then, when I found a place to keep it, I sat and looked at it. Through seeing the worn leather straps and the gold snap fastener on the top, I seemed to gather the courage for the get-away. I planned to leave some morning, and go to the mountains across from our house. Once there, I should find some rock or ledge that I might sleep in, and perhaps the next few days wander through these woods, or go on farther to others more distant, less familiar. I admit my plans were tenuous. Why I planned to leave in the morning instead of at night I do not know. Maybe it was realization of the fact that evening always drew my father and mother and me closer together at home, and that I would be more loathe to leave at that time than in the morning. More likely, it was probably the stark truth that I was afraid of the mystery of the dark and of being alone with that mystery in an unknown woods.

But it was not the plans that counted. It was the idea. It was the idea I dwelt on and feasted on. Looking at the bag, I could already smell the pine needles under my feet in the woods and feel the coldness of that early morning fog on my face. I could already sense the joy of experiencing these moments alone; of thinking uninterruptedly and by myself; of giving way completely to the sensations of nature and of living things. Every day I went to the bag, where it was hidden, and looked at it and gathered strength from it. I dreamed so hard that the dream and the reality blended, and were difficult to separate.

Gradually I put together a few things I was to carry with me in my suitcase, although now I had come to look more on the

Nine

. . . .

bag as an object to take along for its own companionship than for the conveying services it might render. In other words, the bag had become a symbol to me of the whole idea, complete, entire, even to the sensuous enjoyments of eyes and ears and nose. Children are apt to inhabit a world of symbols.

As I said in the beginning, I do not know what happened to my idea that it was never realized in actuality. I imagine Mother found the suitcase, or a rainy spell came; I cannot recall. But somehow, the thinking on it had been enough. There in the bottom of the tan leather bag lay the crackers and cheese I had carried from the kitchen. And the little pencils and a book, and my toothbrush. They seemed small and most insignificant when I looked at them now, with the knowledge that I was not really going away. But before, they had seemed ample and abundant. They had seemed like fit companions for a trip which I took wholly in my own imagination. And so close was the union between mind and body, that I could dream over a musty suitcase and scheme of sleeping in the woods, and dream and sketch so vividly that there was neither disappointment nor frustration in laying aside the actual plans when interference came.

Perhaps it was the common urge to sometimes get away from people that made me want to run away. Perhaps it was a sudden hunger to be alone and feel the presence of the woods. Whatever it was, it tapped the deep roots of my imaginings, and made me believe that somewhere there was something strange and glowing in the forest of time where I might be lost from home and at the same time found.

SHE WAS an old woman who lived in a dingy shack in the valley and went her way without benefit of company. She lived alone. Her cabin stood on the same hill with the church, nearer the road. I cannot remember the first time I saw her or the last. Somehow she became part of the picture, and to remove her from it would be to leave empty a small dark corner. Every community or town has such an old woman. She is frightful to the children, she is repulsive to the grown folks, she is left alone by them all.

One time, there would have been interest in her in certain communities, she would have been a "character," there would have been something fascinating to people about her very difference. But when I was growing up, and since, there has been no interest in distinctive people, unless they became famous or wealthy through their distinctiveness. There was a norm of beauty, a norm of activity, a norm pattern for what went on every-day, and woe be he who swerved away from that norm. His penalty was isolation. That was the old woman's penalty.

Her cabin was unpainted and the years and years of weather had beaten it into a hard dark gray. The roof was shingled with homemade shingles and the yard was beaten hard and grassless with the padding back and forth of her toughened shoeless feet. There were a couple of apple trees between the yard and the road, and they were old too, like everything else. They had never been pruned or cared for, and they rambled in all directions, their branches twisting above the roof of the cabin, making the sagged front entrance seem dark and small between them.

There was a cow and occasionally some chickens. The cow was poor and bony, for it never had a pasture but merely ate from the roadsides and along little patches no one seemed to own or claim. Sometimes the old woman would tie the cow along the road, but more often she would stand and hold the rope herself, waiting for the cow to pick along the grass and move slowly down the narrow strip beside the pavement. They were there often in the summer, and as we passed by, I would stare at the old woman with a tense curiosity. Her cow with its gaunt sides, picking hungrily at the thin dry grasses which grow between road and fence, and she standing near, holding the rope in her hand and moving a snuff stick slowly back and forth in her mouth, watching the cars which occasionally passed, with an impenetrable stare.

She always had a snuff stick in her mouth, and snuff ran along her lips and sometimes down her chin. She was very dirty. Her feet in the summertime were the color of earth and the old shingles combined, for she went barefooted the entire summer and never washed her feet. The dresses she wore were long and loose; I do not recall them very well. Her hair was gray and straggly, and her face was broad and finely lined. A web of lines crisscrossed over her forehead, and ran down her cheeks, beside her eyes which were blue and sharp. The sharpness was a surprise, for it came unexpectedly in the face so out of keeping.

Not far from where she lived, a girl my own age lived, and we became curious about the old woman and the house she lived in. How we came to go down and see her, not once but several times, I do not know. But go we did, and she welcomed us. I cannot separate any of those times in my mind, they are all too blurred together, but I do remember once in the spring when we went there and she had a tiny bunch of violets in a vase; once when we went into her kitchen and saw the flies so thick on a churning of butter she had made that we were sick with the sight; once when she told us she didn't go to Sunday School like we did because if God was so all-powerful why didn't he do away with the devil? Then if God had made the world where did he come from in the first place? I admit we were no help to her questions, for certainly we didn't know the answers and we were no end shocked anyway. I remember after that sitting in the church window once or twice, while the minister was preaching, and I would see the old woman with her cow down along the edge of other people's pastures, standing there in the sunshine, each moving so slowly it was difficult to see the actual motion, only the accomplished act. Or—I would see her down in her little yard, below the church, stirring about on some task unknown to me, with the sound of bees and summer bugs loud around her, and the sweet smell of locusts or honeysuckle in the air. She appeared to me as we must have appeared to whatever spirit sat above watching us—far-away, very small, and infinitely pitiful.

The one time I distinctly remember, above all others, of being at the old woman's cabin, was one morning when she took us up to her attic. In reality, it was supposed to be the third room of the house, for the two rooms downstairs were her living-bedroom and kitchen. Now it was a store room, an attic, though most would wonder what an old woman like she was would have to store. The steps were little more than a wooden ladder; we had read about cobwebs and dusky places in adventure books, but in reality they were not so picturesque, merely bothersome. There was the small room, so low she had to stoop below the roof, but we were small anyway and could stand upright. It came about that she had brought us here to show us her treasures. We were disappointed. How small they seemed. How worthless they looked. A few bits of furniture, a picture or two, some odds and ends of china, and glass, and over in one corner books. There were many books, piled in high uneven stacks under the eaves. She picked up a small blue cup.

"My girl used to like this cup, when she was a little girl, like you are," and she handled it gently.

Her hands were dirty to the point of filth along the china and the glass. She talked in a low voice, falling more and more into herself, forgetting us in the moment of these things. We watched her a little contemptuously. This was a dirty old woman with some things that looked more like the junk-pile than anything else. We looked about us curiously, hoping for something else, for something more spectacular, wishing even the book-backs looked readable and not so forlorn. But there was nothing else. Here before us, scattered on the floor, lay all there was. It was not half so much as we thought it would be.

Mumbling, fingering each object carefully as if it had its own separate reason for being, she went on for a little while. Then she looked up and it struck her like a blow that we were neither listening nor caring about what she might say. She saw our disappointment in the poverty of what we had hoped would be a hidden treasure. Her keen eyes looked at us for an unforgettable moment. Then she raised herself from the floor and stood as erect as she could under the rafters. It was as if she might have said to us, "It was not half so much as I once thought it would be, either."

We followed her downstairs. Both of us were uncomfortable for we suddenly realized that she had been showing us a sort of harvest, the reaping of something we could not realize, could only vaguely sense. We left soon.

After that I learned that she had loved a man once, had in fact borne a baby, and that she had read all the books she owned and many more. The glass and china we had seen in her attic were supposedly antiques.

"Law's have mercy," the mother of the little girl who had gone with me said. "Why didn't you ask her for some of it? I'll bet you didn't even let on you cared, and she'd probably have given you some too." She probably would have. Certainly we hadn't let on we cared. But our deepest regrets were for another kind of caring that we had failed to show.

We did not go back to the old woman's house again. It would have embarrassed us too much, and embarrassed her, I believe. She had tried to give us something and she had tried to find something in us. We had failed in both cases, and it is hard to rewind old threads.

I still saw her along the road in summer, or around her yard in the winter, and she became as constant as a landmark. Then one day she went away. Went to live with her daughter finally; the house was destroyed. For awhile the apple trees stood, their long branches seeming empty and ghost-like on moonlit nights. Later on they were cut down too, but that was after I was grown and the old woman had been buried in my memory under a silt of accumulating days.

THERE ARE SOME who think of nature in terms of only one special sort of beauty. It is the beauty of a tree bursting green with the springtime; or the beauty of a robin hopping along the ground after a shower; or a flower blossoming in some unexpected corner of the woods. These are the prettier evidences of beauty in nature. But they are not grand. They lack a quality we find in the darker aspects of a natural world which is not always pleasant or pretty.

The year I was nine, there was a forest fire on the mountain opposite our house. Where or how it started we did not know, but suddenly there were billowing puffs of smoke along the sky, and the puffs stretched like clouds into long thin wisps and finally melted into distance. It was far away on the tops of the hills when it began, and we were told of the men who had gone to fight the fire. Sometimes they would go up by our house during the day, and straggle down later, with their shirts wet with sweat and their faces black with smoke. The smell of the smoke began to fill the air, bitter and fragrant with the odors of many burning trees, pine, oak, chestnut, maple. The men could not stop the fire, however; they could only attempt to control it, and by the second and third day, it had reached closer to our house. Now we could hear trees falling all along the mountainside, and the smoke was curling thick and blue against the sky. Now and then a man would tell us of the little animals he had seen running away from the fire: rabbits and foxes and all the creatures which hid between the big grey stones, and in the hollow logs and in the trees which had seemed so tall and safe.

The fire was put out, but it had burned for almost a week. Men had seemed helpless before it, but they had not been helpless, for in the end they had succeeded and the waste was stopped. The fire had singed their hair and eyebrows, the cinders and ashes had been hot beneath their feet, and the breath of the fire had been hot against them, but they had won, in the end. We had sat below and watched the fire and seen the men go up and down the road, to and from it, and there had been something extraordinarily beautiful about it all.

The first slow warning smoke along the sky; the gradual cumulation until it grew near to us and hung heavy over the

Nine

head of the valley; the sounds of the trees crashing, splintering to the ground in an echoing burst, and then the quieter steadier crackle of the moving fire which overcame the greater sound as smaller steadier things often overcame the greater: all of these were beautiful. It was a terrible, wasteful sight to watch the trees and the fire, but its very alienism was a fascination, and its transience made it precious. I could think of the animals running before it, their eyes bright with fear, and terror lending swiftness to the running. Even the snakes, the long, cold-blooded snakes so wary of this inferno, they were exciting to think on. With what soundless undulations, with what uncanny rhythm and speed, must they slide from the sections of cliff-like rocks and race away before the approaching fire.

Certainly this was not a pretty thing—this forest fire. But it held a deep nocturnal beauty which was somehow more gripping and more awful than any lovely thing. After the fire had gone, and the smoke and smell of burning leaves and timber had disappeared, there remained the black earth and the black tree trunks where the fire had been. It was easy to tell the lines of beginning and ending. The larger trees which had fallen could still be seen as charred logs stretched along the ground. And the trees which stood were mostly dead, or burned so that they soon would die. The black seemed very dark against the blue sky, and the greenness of the other mountains seemed even greener beside the black. It was surprising to look toward the woods and see only stark barrenness, with nothing to cover the nakedness of the earth underneath. All the ferns, the shrubs, the laurel and azalea bushes, the galax and the woods flowers, had been consumed completely. But the remembrance of the red flames among the green and brown of the hillside, the odors and the sounds, and the terrifying presence of a familiar thing gone wild, of a common force unharnessed and primitive, these were beautiful in their dark terror.

....

ten

....

NORTH CAROLINA is a long state, running five hundred and twenty miles from coast to mountains, but not quite half as wide, only two hundred miles from the northern boundary of Virginia to the southern boundaries of South Carolina and Georgia. Driving the length of this state is an experience in geography and in human nature. For it includes the western mountaineers and the eastern coast-people, the mountain twang and the low drawl of the negro.

My Aunt Maude moved to this eastern part of the state, near Raleigh, when I was ten years old, and one week-end we drove down to see her. Leaving the mountains, how wide the country flattened out, like a roll of paper gradually unrolled and made level. Scrub pines were the usual trees along the road, and the earth became redder, shading off in places to a white color. Sometimes we saw a long-leafed pine, and the first of these was a surprise to me. They were different from our white and black pines in the mountains, and had longer needles dripping from their branches, as the name would indicate. There were no patches of dark woods along the way, nor any cold hidden creeks. Here in the openness, there was no secret spot, no hidden view, where rounding a curve, one might suddenly come upon the green presence of rhododendron and laurel and blooming azalea.

Yet there was a width to the horizon, a roundness like the flat face of the moon which was edged with light and yet remained edgeless, sloped off into the distance where we could not follow. The sun seemed closer too, and we more exposed to it. Certainly there was a languor in the air that one could never feel at home in the mountains.

Along the road there were many negroes now, moving slowly on foot, or in rickety wagons which were patched with wire and other miscellany. I had never seen so many mules before. Every wagon seemed to be pulled by a mule which suited its pace to the heat and its own empty sides. Most of the cabins were unpainted along the road; the weather had brought to them all a common color, and there was a certain unity in their very shack-like appearance. The lack of paint disturbed my father a great deal. Even some of the better built and more prosperous houses in the country were unpainted and had stood so for many years.

Through the towns there was a slower tempo, too. A tempo in keeping with the sun. How short a distance we had to come, a couple of hundred miles, not even a whole day's driving, and not only the land and the horizon had changed but the people and the towns, too.

My aunt lived in a village near Raleigh, our state capital. Sleeping there was the first time I had ever slept near the sound of a train in the night. It was a lonely and forsaken sound, filling the night with its whistle and the roar of its turning wheels, beating like the nerve of this great sleeping giant of a country as it rushed on through the darkness. The whistle cry, with its rising and falling cadences, came across the broad flatness, echoed through the quietness of the sleeping village and darkened houses, and faded away across the summer stillness of the night.

In the morning the sun was a red flame in the east. I had never seen anything like it before. Round and glowing as if with the heat of a single orange-yellow coal it appeared suddenly, boldly against the rim of sky. Morning had come. With none of the mist or slanting rays or reflected light of the hills, morning here had come with no forewarning, no debate of shadows. Every day

I watched this rising of the sun. The fig bushes and the muscadine vines stood grey beside the brilliance of its red.

As to the muscadines, Aunt Maude said, "You ought to smell them when they're ripe. Why, I've walked out in the little patch of woods there many a time, and found them by their smell. Great big, sweet grapes hanging ripe and rotting. The smell of muscadines is just like wine."

Coming home, the pattern was just opposite from what it had been driving down. First there were the open spaces, then the low hills in the distance, and then all at once we were in the mountains, among them. There were ravines below us along the road, and above us were trees and underbushes climbing along the mountainsides. The sky was only a patch of blue, and we seemed very small beneath it. We were home.

THE GARDEN we planted had many enemies. There were the things in the ground, on the ground, and above the ground. Sometimes in the spring we would go out and find the tiny green sprouts we had tended so carefully and watched so sharply, cut off at the ground. Along a whole row, maybe two, it would be the same. The cut-worms had come. Once in awhile my mother would dig into the earth around the root, her eyes burning over the row of ruined green sprouts, and there the worm would be. She would mash it to death on a rock. Usually the worm was not there. Finding them always made me think of a tree Aunt Maude had cut in her yard once. We found in the decaying heart and trunk of the tree, great round things that looked like a combination of a large worm and a snail. Slugs, someone said they were, and it seemed like a good name. The sound of it went right with their heavy sluggish-looking thickness. My aunt took the slugs out of the tree and burned them. She said it was the only way they could be killed for sure. The tree had looked so solid and so healthy standing we could hardly believe these had been at its core.

Rabbits sometimes came to the garden too, and during the night would eat off the budding plants of vegetables or flowers.

They were very daring once in awhile, and came during the day. We would look out of our kitchen window, over the flower-bed, and see one hopping along, nibbling with swift jerky bites on the succulent sprouts. Or we might see one in the garden from our front porch. Whenever I saw one I would not tell of it, but watch it as close as I might, and let it eat as much as it would. I didn't think that it was eating my food as certainly as if it had eaten from a plate I had fixed; but if hunger had been a more pressing element in our days, I would have killed the little fluffy-tailed thing, and gladly. It was serving its stomach and I would have served mine. As it was, I could afford generosity and free-ness of spirit.

There were blights, too, which came on certain vegetables, and laid waste as completely as insect or animal. There was less satisfaction in combating blight for it was seemingly a more inanimate enemy and less spectacular in its death. But there were constant sprays and powders to be used; we had a small hand spray which was ornery to use, for one nozzle kept insisting on poking its head out of the solution. So I went along and helped by holding this nozzle down in the bucket. Mother or my father would pump vigorously on the handles, scattering a mist of liquid over the leaves and leaving drops of white over the green leaves of maybe a potato plant. This spray on potatoes and beans was for bugs too, small hard brilliant things, colored vivid orange with black dots on their back. Nature made even her smallest ambassadors with a perfect pattern and a harmony of color. When the spray went on the leaves, I was happy that here was health for the plant, even if some other bit of life had to die. But that was the way all around: birth and growth feasted on death, and in the end, death was triumphant over all except the earth. The earth gave new promise every spring, and the seasons continued their coming and going. The birds moulted and their life was a moment, the animals preyed on one another and in turn found their attacker, people grew grey with stiffened muscles and tasted the dust. Only the moon rode high and clear,

remote from death; only the stars shone cold and forever mysterious and knew no end; only the earth turned in its giant fertility
and tasted no pangs of a probable death.

These things I could think on when I saw a worm or a rabbit. They were strange revealing thoughts which plunged me
into inconspicuousness in the universe. But I was ten and life
seemed centuries long before me. The earth was around me and
I was upon it. My spindly legs perhaps were none too firmly set,
but certainly they were planted with determination and spirit. I
meant to feel the sun and watch spring in the garden, to come
as close as I could to the wary rabbits and the animals which
crossed our yard in the night and left footprints in the yielding
snow.

THE ROAD which ran in front of our house was an interesting
tributary to our life. When it was first made, when my father had
seen it first and when my mother had moved there as a girl, it was
a shaded winding road which was little more than a lane. Giant
oaks and maples and chestnuts stood along it, holding the sun
in summer and making a pleasant green-lit shade. Even when I
was first born, when my [half] sister [Helen Dykeman] took me
on our horse and we rode, when I was so small she had to hold
me tightly on the saddle, along the road, it was thick along each
side with trees. How quickly they have gone, once started. Now
it is simply a graveled road leading to the main highway, standing open to the sun in summer and the whipping wind in winter.
But the people still go along the road, and though not as numer-
ous as they once were because of the national parkway which
has given them a new way to their homes across the mountain,
they are surprisingly the same as they have always been.

The mountain farmers are not large of wife or barn or storehouse. Their women are more often thin and stooped than
buxom; they hold their arms, not wide at their sides, but folded
tightly across their breasts. Their barns are usually unpainted,
poor affairs, with little else to use them than a cow whose ribs

Ten

....

are easily numbered under her skin, or an occasional mule who is too slow, or underfed, to be worth the effort of harnessing. It is a meagre existence they lead, such an existence as gives them a narrow special outlook on the world. But their springs burst clear and cold from the hills and their air is rarefied and pure— little else do they ask of life.

Often we used to see these people passing along the road, on their way to or from the town. Sometimes they went by at nightfall, carrying heavy loads on their shoulders, weighted down with food—coffee, meal, and lard their main purchases—and various store-bought goods. We used to talk with these travelers, stopping one now and then on the road, as we might see him.

One of these characters was an old bent man who always made me think of some magician in a dusty book, or a sorcerer in an ancient tale. He was dark, with long shaggy hair under his shapeless hat, and he wore a black coat which hung loosely down over his stooped back and flapped open at the front. He always carried a little leather bag with him—one of those old fashioned hand-bags of tough leather that was worn with wear and faded into an unidentifiable color. To complete the picture, he used a long walking stick, the end of which rose higher than his head and provided a peculiar contrast to his bentness. Seeing him walk along the road, as he placed the tall straight stick before him and then drew himself toward it, gave a strange impression. Like a man grasping hold on a straw. Like the whole race of these mountain men, constantly aware of their frailty beside the trees and stones.

As I say, I used to watch this man with hungry curiosity—he was someone from a story-book, someone unreal and fictional. But my mother talked with him. She was always interested in the odd people, those who were unlike the common types who always resembled an advertisement for cosmetics or tooth-paste or some certain brand of clothes. These people found their standards through some promoter's ads or through some manufacturer's picture of what the correct person should wear or be. Mother was not interested in such walking billboards. "They're all the same," she said. But let some likeable mountaineer woman live nearby, or let someone she knew to be out of the ordinary pass by, and how she could talk with them. There was a gentleness, a genuine interest about the way she met people, that put them off their usual guard at once.

So many of the people I have known today want only to become acquainted with people who fit into an already conceived pattern which has been set up in their mind's eye. Mother was interested in all patterns and especially in one she had not thought of before. The unique, the different, in character interested her. And after all, what does the word character mean but that each of us should be startlingly different in our temperaments and ways of life. Perhaps we are different, underneath, but how scared we are to appear individual outwardly. Surely there are few enough original people in the world, and we cannot afford to overlook those few.

To get on with my man, he was often going by our house, and I remember he sat down to rest near our gate late one afternoon. Mother and I talked with him, at least Mother did, and I listened. I stared at the greasy little satchel and wondered what it carried. Finally he must have seen me staring. "Hit's my yerbs," he said, pointing with the stick toward the satchel he had set beside him. "I'm a yerb doctor."

"And you can carry all your herbs around with you in your little bag," Mother said. I knew she had spoken so that I'd know what the man meant when he said yerbs. "What can you cure with your herbs?"

"'Bout ary ailment a-body's likely to have," he answered. "Why, I've been so good with these here yerbs that the big fine doctors in town are all jealous over hit. That's jest the reason I don't try to do more than I do, I hate to run them out of business." He paused a moment, his eyes alert for our reactions, of belief or unbelief in his tale. "Of course," he went on, "they've

Ten

....

113

been to all these big fine schools and learned to write a lot of Latin words. But I kin read Latin. Didn't know that did you?" and he chuckled in little high-pitched jerks. "Yessir, I kin read Latin, and I kin tell what they air puttin' in their big fine doses of medicine. An' hit ain't no more nor no less than I kin make right out o' my yerbs. They come right out o' the ground, too, and they air puore and filled with healing as the airth and the Lord can make 'em. Yessir, I'd a-sight ruther trust these here yerbs than the little pink waters and pills the city doctors gives."

Most certainly there was something in what he said. But when he opened his bag and showed us the little dried up bundles of roots, and leaves, tied with dirty string and dusty from years of handling and carrying, his arguments lost their savor.

Another time he told us of an adventure he had had during the Civil War. "Now I war'nt in many big fights, the ones listed down in the hist'ry books and all, but I was in some might fierce skirmishes. And you know, the skirmishes was sometimes as bad as the battles. Why, lots of times they was a heap worse than the battles. Yessir, they was. A heap worse. Well, anyway, I did some mighty rough fightin' in those skirmishes, and they got to callin' me The Cap, which was short for Captain. I'd jest laugh an' go on with my fightin' whenever anybody started funnin' and said somethin' about The Cap. Well, one day we got in a mighty hot little set-to. It was us or them and hand to hand fightin' all the way. Durin' the course of the fightin' word started out through our men that The Cap had been killed. Well sirs, you never seen nothin' like it. They started breakin' up, our men did, an' it was somethin' scary. They jest throwed their guns and all to the ground and started leavin'. Seems like the heart had jest gone out of 'em. Jest about the time it was really lookin' bad though, word came back along the lines, 'The Cap still lives.' Right thar them men picked up their guns and went into that fight, and by gum if we didn't lick the tar outen those others. Yessir," and he looked away down the road as if he could see the faces of each of those men, "it was jest 'bout one of the most godsent little tributes I ever had paid me."

"Do you sp'ose it really happened?" I asked Mother afterward.

"No," she said. "He wasn't even in the Civil War probably." I was disappointed. "But," she went on, "where else would you find an old man with an imagination like that? I think it's a better story if he made it up than if it really happened."

That's the way Mother was about people.

SOMETIMES IN THE MORNING I would be awakened by the sound of our churn downstairs. It was a small daisy churn which required hand turning, and my father usually elected himself to the task of turning the crank. There was something about the steady motion, the feel of the swish of cream under his hand, the necessity of patience, that lent itself to his manipulation.

Mother skimmed the cream from extra milk we had—thick, dry-looking ropes of cream they were—and left it to stand in a grey crock until it had soured and could be churned. The churning itself would have been a chore for us if we had not enjoyed it so much. There was always an eagerness to see just how much butter would be made, and then there was the satisfaction of having made food for one's self, independent of the stores and their little square boxes.

There was an art to gathering the butter after the churning itself was finished. It took a slow jerking back and forth of the dasher to make all the yellow particles stick together and form a sort of ball which could be picked up with the round old wooden ladle. There was a wooden bowl, too, to match the ladle, and in that Mother pressed and worked out all the buttermilk which still stood in the butter. When all that remained was a yellow solid mass, she salted it, then molded it into the pound and half-pound prints. The pound print had two flowers which came out on the butter like a natural design; and the half-pound print had a pattern which covered the whole top of the butter pat with circles and little triangles. There was a sweet smell to the butter when it came out of the wooden prints which had been scalded and scrubbed so often that the brown natural wood color was glossed over with a whiteness from steam and soap and water.

The buttermilk was really something to taste! Tiny yellow flecks of butter floated on the surface and filled the mouth with beads of sweetness. This was summer clover and grass and winter oats made into nectar for those who would take the trouble . . .

I DO NOT KNOW when I first began writing poetry. I only know that by the time I was ten I had a sheaf of ill-penned poems carefully hidden in a tin box. Their subject matter ranged from churning and vivid descriptions of the fresh butter and buttermilk, to evening sunsets and rippling streams. There seemed to be so little distinction in my mind between what was considered poetical and what was not. Anything which appealed to my senses, whether through touch, sight, smell, taste, or hearing, was good enough for me, and I could compose a verse for it.

My father and mother always encouraged me in these verses. They often read poetry to me, and my father was a master at quoting many of the older poets and many of the old classics. Sir Water Scott was one of his favorites, and I can hear his voice now, as he would quote side after side of "Marmion." And at that line, "Burn'd Marmion's swarthy cheek like fire," my father's cheeks, and mine too, were burning with the intensity of the poem.

The first poem I ever wrote and showed to anyone except my mother or my father, was mostly written by my father. He stood in front of the window one morning, looking out on the hill, and he said, "Little girl, why don't you write a poem about what you can see from this window?" He stood for a moment, thoughtful, then he gave me some of the lines. I forget them now, but they were of the galax and the ferns and all the life that lived in that narrow patch of hill I could see from my bedroom window. That was what we named the poem: "From My Bedroom Window." It told of what I had seen, and what my father had helped me to see; and it also gave me the spirit and desire for other poems,

Ten

....

116

ones which I should make up by myself, and which would hint of other windows.

There was great joy to me in writing those little poems. I had no standards of criticism, I had no fear of triteness or any other of the hundred besetting sins, and I wrote for myself, not for others. I had something I wanted to say, and if I could only put it on paper my impulse was satisfied. It was a glorious, vigorous impulse. Sometimes it came over me in one burst of thought or feeling, and I was exalted, made happy and unreal by it. Then I must do more than write down words. I must run or leap or shout against the air until my breath was fast and the blood in my body was faster. Then I could fall down on the ground, feel the earth's coolness and warmth, and find that though my body was exhausted, my mind and my spirit went on leaping forward toward the wind, singing and throwing their song toward the mountains.

Other times, such feelings would come slowly, like a mysterious accumulation of good things all through the day. There was the joy of waking and finding a new day; there was always the joy of waking and wondering what all the stretching unknown hours would roll before me. But on these mornings there was special joy, like a warm soft light inside myself. Through breakfast and the morning, the light would glow, and burn higher and higher, growing subtly and surely on every triviality, every little goodness. Then the flame would burst forth, no longer a glow but a beautiful fire, and I would feel as if the world were small and bound with circling bands. I would feel as if there were some word I must say, some song I must sing, in order that my pitch of feeling might grow infectious, and I could plant it like a living germ in every person that I met. It was a heady delirium, lyric with the pulse of childhood.

Whatever became of those poems, I do not know. I wonder if it matters. And I have wondered since if all the glory of those impulses must be lost in us because we do not know the words or forms wherein to capture them. It is an ironical fact that when

Ten

....

117

we are young and taste the fire, we lack the techniques and the artistic modes for expressing ourselves. And when we are older and know the techniques and modes, then we have lost the leaping flame of that first fire.

CHRISTMAS AGAIN, and snow this year! The air filled with movement of innumerable flakes falling in steady rhythm to the ground, covering each object impartially, completely. Ah, how the snow excited me. Each time it came it was something new to me, as if it came the first time I had ever seen it fall; the sharp edge of wonder never dulled by having seen the whiteness before. It was always different, always beautiful.

And who has said the snow is silent? For ears accustomed to silence, the snow is sound. The faint murmur of the flakes piling one on top of the other fills the woods, and the leaves and stones and lichens are sounding boards for the snow, responding to its infinitesimal weight. It is far lonelier than silence to stand alone in the woods and hear the small noises of the snow. There is a hush, a mystic quality about those very sounds that gives to winter a freedom from lush sensation and feeling that is difficult to know during any other season in the woods.

Now is the time when each small thing comes into its own perfection. The blade of broomsedge weed is no less than the limb of the great white pine, for each is covered with its burden of snow, and each is transformed in its own magic. How unbelievable to me that every brown weed has its lacy pattern of ice and snow—how inconceivable that nothing should have been overlooked.

How beautiful even man's botches have become under the snow. The broken gates, the sagging fences, the neglected yards and pastures: now they are right, are interesting of shape under the snow. It is an interval time of kindness. It is a time of undulation and curving softness. Fall is supposed to be the time of luxuriance, but it seems to me this is no less a time of fullness. Snow gives a quality of sweep to the mountains, a connectedness and oneness that subtracts the sharper peaks and banks, which are usually dominant, into a part of the curve made by all the mountains and streams. The branches of the trees are curved, the weeds and grasses bend toward the ground in the weight of the snow, roof peaks on the houses are round and no longer cut against the sky.

Daddy and I went out each Christmas to bring the Christmas tree home together. It was a great feat, picking the tree, searching for it, finding one whose removal would not mean too great a loss to the woods.

Our dog went along, leaping through the still woods, hoping to start a rabbit, running back now and then to see after us. My father always took his little axe, carrying it on his shoulder. The rosin of the cut pine was always thick and sticky, but the odor was fresh and good as any perfume to me. It was quite a ritual, this bringing of the tree. And the years it snowed, how much more real and memorable was the task. For during the year I have just mentioned, there was that perfection, large and small, that seeming newness of the earth, which made the winter best of all the seasons: earth waiting to be reborn.

eleven

S UMMERTIME. The days endless, stretching between sunrise and dark like the languid unrolling of some interminable carpet. The chickens fluffed their wings in the afternoon dust and turned a gray color over the natural red of their feathers. The mourning dove cooed low and melodious in the woods.

"That's a sign of rain," my mother said.

The mournful quietness of the dove's voice would blend with the warmth and stillness of the afternoon when scarcely a leaf shivered on any tree and the sky was solid blue above the rim of the mountains.

Such were the days when I could lie in the sun on the hot grass, burning my legs and back to a hickory-nut tan, and watch the comings and goings of the butterflies which crowded around our summer lilac bush. They drifted and circled over the bending lavender flowers and when they lighted, seemed merely to touch the petals. Their wings folded and unfolded as they sat there, relieved for a moment from their perpetual flutterings.

I found a book on butterflies and saved some money which I sent to a nature institute for a dozen or so life-size pictures of butterflies which they sent me. Seeing them on the lilac in the yard was not enough for me—I must know about them. About their habits, the span of their lives, how they were made, and most of all—their names. At last, I decided to make myself a net and sacrifice one butterfly of each type to my urge for knowledge and possession.

It was a far-flung enterprise I had undertaken, but there was some essence of pursuit after pure fantasy that surrounded me as I ran over the fields or waited patiently in the garden or woods while one of my coquettish prizes decided where to light. I raced through pastures white with blooming daisies, through the hot garden where our vegetables grew so patiently; I cut my legs with the briars and tangles in the daisies—but always there was flitting before me that bit of color.

My beginning was ostentatious. I caught a tiger swallow-tail. How large it seemed, lying dead in my hand. And I had not realized before the balance of the design it wore: the black bars forming a pattern across the yellow of its wings and the outline of those wings following so symmetrical a pattern culminating in the tails which gave it its name.

Then there was a monarch, orange-rust colored and traced with black again—a male and female; a black swallow-tail with splotches of blue and a bit of red; and a little white cabbage butterfly and all its brilliant sulphur relations of yellow and orange and variations of those colors.

Most of my butterflies had slender long bodies, wore pointer-like antennae, and flew during the daylight. But when I branched out to moths, as I soon did, I found they were plumper and shorter of body, wore plumed antennae and flew at night. One of my first moths was the quite familiar Cecropia. Its body was thick, colored orange and striped with tan and white. Its wings were a beige color shading to tan, with orange and white and brownish stripes around the edges. On each of the four wings was a small half moon of orange, and in each of the far upper corners of the two front wings was a blue-black circle—fine relief to the solid effect of orange and tan. Something alike was the Polyphemus moth— golden tan, distinguished by ovals on its lower wings. These ovals were bluish in color with a touch of red and blue inside that made them look like the pupil of some ever-focused eye.

Enough of the big names which I learned and never seemed to tire of. They permitted me to know my moths and butterflies,

Eleven

separate them in my mind, and keep them as individuals. My swallow-tail, which had had a bit of the color brushed off his left wing, was quite real to me. I regretted the loss of any particle of the bright dust on his plumage.

But my collection would not have been complete until I captured the prima donna of moths—that most fragile of the fragile—a luna moth. Even its name held certain intimations for me, the cool remoteness of the moon.

So, I hunted for a specimen, waiting, searching, worrying.

Then one night I went upstairs to bed, and there in the bathroom, lying on the white shining surface of the bathtub, was my luna moth. Its forewings were spread in all the perfectness of their symmetry, and from beneath these forewings came the indented sweep of those matchless wings underneath. These wings were wide at the top, corresponding with those above, but further down they sloped gradually to slender swallow-like tails. Poised and beautiful beyond description they lay motionless, having been made for motion—caught in a moment when life had just gone and death was yet hardly present. I shall not forget the green so pale it bordered on white of the moth's wings, or the soft fur-like yellowness of its body, or those four matched dots, one on each wing, of yellow, white, and brown.

The porcelain of the bathtub seemed harsh, its white glare was brazen, against this premier which nature and the night had settled here. And after all my searching and fretting it had come in this least of all likely places and manners—from where we could not tell. It was a slight piece of perfection dropped among us, and I felt a delicious thrill before the perfectness. My father and mother felt this too, and spoke of the luna moth as if they, too, considered it worthy of all the attention I showered on it. I did not realize how much I appreciated their kindred feelings. Not until later, when I met people who swatted at moths, who could not find time to study such color, and who left me alone in my world of small beauties.

....

I mounted my moths and butterflies with the luna moth at the center. Under the cotton I hid tobacco leaves and other preventives against the small destroyers which might crawl inside my case and eat their kinsfolk. When I was finished, they lay like a spilled rainbow under the glass.

So they remained for several years. Then one day I found them almost destroyed. It had happened quickly, for the case was where I could see it often. But the tender bodies were partially gone, the wings broken, eaten away. Little was left of all the glorious color. Dust to dust.

AT THE MOUTH of the valley where we lived stood a white framed church. It was situated on a sort of promontory through which the pavement highway cut. On the right hand side was a hill where the church sat. On the other side, a house sat; then the hill fell away sharply to the creek which wound around at its base.

It was a unique church, and one of my earliest memories. The backbone rafter of its roof sloped in rhythm with the red and broom-sedge hill. Its clear sharp sides seemed to deny such harmony with the earth, however, and rose in a vertical cut against the sky. There was a pointed steeple, the only ornamental touch. And even it had acquired through the years a utilitarian look, almost as if ashamed to stand in solemn ornamental pose when all around it served a cause.

Around the curve, and there before us lay the valley, and driving up it we could look toward the mountains and tell which peak was ours, which hill stood behind our house.

Before I started to school, this church and Sunday School provided my main social life. My father seldom went to church. He stayed at home and read or walked. His observance of Sunday was simply a day of quiet. But for myself, I looked forward to Sunday School and Mother taking me. It was the time when I could see people my own age—or people of any age would do, for that matter—and when I could mix and mingle. I was alone enough during the week—I wanted to talk now, I wanted to find out about people. And I did. I talked in the Sunday School class, I wiggled on the church benches, I wrote notes on the sides of my quarterly and passed them along the row for answers.

Churches play this role in the lives of many mountain people, or in the lives of many country folks all over the country, who do not get together often except for church and who want to keep up with the happenings of the community. I have seen mountain churches where the men stood outside in the yard during the entire service, their hands in the pockets of their best overalls, or more often busy whittling on a random stick, while they squatted on the ground or leaned against the trees, and compared crops and prices and trades of the week.

Our church was only a few minutes from town, however, and any of the members could have gone to one of the more impressive, expensive churches in the city if they had wished. They remained here, however, in a church reminiscent of a history in which they had played a part, and might still play such a part. There was a ruggedness, and lack of fabulous ornateness found in some of the others, that made them more comfortable in this plain church.

There are certain pictures in the memory of that church that follow from my second or third year through my first teens. One is the communion: the white linen cloth covering the silver plates and glass wine cups. This cloth always had four distinct creases in it and folded easily in the minister's hand when he lifted it from the table. The mouths slowly chewing in unison on a bit of dry cracker, then swallowing, and all the throats moving rhythmically. The tinkle that the glasses made when they were set back in the silver cases which the deacons passed. It seemed so loud in the almost breathless church. Another girl and I formed the habit of rushing up after communion, when we were hardly high enough to manipulate the covers, and drink the grape juice that was left in any of the untouched glasses.

Then one of the missionary ladies protested against what she called our sacrilege. We could not understand her reasoning, for the moment had passed when the drink had been special, and what remained was only sweet juice from last summer's grapes. Mother did not permit me to drink anymore, however.

Another picture I know by heart was the taking of collection. How slowly the deacons would go forward, the floor creaking vaguely under the weight of some of them. There they would stand before the table with their heads bowed while the preacher prayed. I guess I didn't hear many of those prayers, for I was always so busy looking at the deacons' hands, clasped behind their backs. One of the men was a carpenter and house-painter. There was usually a faint rim of color around his fingernails, telltale of the house he had worked on that week. His hands were worn of the weather, sometimes he would have a mashed thumb, or hurt wrist. Once his little fingernail came off and left a stub of puckered flesh until another nail could grow.

Another of the deacons was a man who ran a feed-store. His hands were fleshy and unstained. They corresponded with the soft sacks of feed which he handled during the week.

The most interesting hands belonged of course to the most interesting man. They were thin knotty hands, reddened with much washing and chapped with the cold. There was the hardness of muscle in the way the fingers clasped one another loosely, yet firmly. This was the deacon whose father had founded the church years before in the 1800s. The old man had come from England when he was young, had settled in this very valley, and had turned much of the ground which had only then been denuded of its tall timber. The ground had yielded stubbornly to the plow, resisting at every thrust with its stones and tangled roots. But he had been stubborn, had succeeded in wrenching a crop from the new ground, and had even planted apple and fruit trees on the slopes.

"I remember my father when I was a boy," this deacon would tell my father. "He would walk over his fields eating fruit, maybe a peach or two. And every seed he had he would plant it beside a stump. He did it so often that finally we had a peach tree growing by almost every stump. Of course, the land wasn't so good for peaches then, but they grew anyway." Another time, he was telling the history of the church to our congregation: "As time went on and the community grew more, and other families lived near, my father decided there should be a church. So he and another man cleared the ground right here. I recall that I was just a boy at the time, and they made me help. This right here where our church stands was the worst patch of thorn bushes I believe I nearly ever saw. Tough, good gracious! And so many of them it seemed impossible that we would ever finish."

Some of the children on the benches were asleep; the women looked unconcerned, with a worry in their minds about the Sunday dinner. One of his fellow deacons, the one with the fleshy hands, nodded heavily in the corner. But he went on talking, telling earnestly of this particle of history which spread out to include a whole era and made a whole generation of people come alive. It seemed so far in the past—few could realize how close in the matter of years it had been to this very day.

"Well then, we got the land cleared and graded, and my father began digging the foundation. But he saw he was going to need someone to help him and so he told the other few men who lived in the community that if they wanted to help, he would contribute all the trees for lumber that they needed. Of course, trees were more plentiful then than they are now, but most people were selling their lumber logs for money. My father gave the lumber for this building.

"I helped cut some of the trees too, long poplars and oaks and walnuts for the benches here. We even made the benches, too. And I remember just as well when we were building it, a man came riding along the road down there one day, of course it was nothing but a dirt buggy lane then with shade trees on either side, but this man came along and saw us working, and he stopped. He watched a few minutes then he called to us, said hello, asked what we were doing. Well, my father told him and he stood there a minute longer, then reached in his pocket and gave us ten dollars. Ten dollars was a lot more money then than it is now. It helped us out.

"Well in May the church was finished and we were ready for our first sermon. We sent over the mountain and got a man we all knew to come and talk to us. We didn't have preaching but one Sunday a month for a good many years—the preachers were on a kind of circuit."

Everyone was restless to leave. They felt no sense of the pastness of life, of the earnest history which this man had lived and could tell about. He went to his seat and sat down. He did not look about him, but toward the pulpit which he had helped to build. He sat with his farmer's hands in his lap, for he had worked with the land his father had cleared, and he had made it earn a living for him, too. Not only a living, but some extra. The extra he saved and gave to foreign mission, and to a small Baptist college near. All this before he had a bathroom in his house, and never yet, any electricity.

The minister at the church when I was very young was a professor of religion in the small college not far from Asheville, to which our deacon had given so much [Mars Hill College]. He was a nervous, small man with iron-grey curly hair, a hobby of photography, and a warm sympathy for the whole race of humanity. I do not remember any of his sermons, which were more talks than sermons, but I do remember his frequent laughter and good humor. On the cold winter Sundays when there were merely a handful of the usual people huddled informally around the roaring pot-bellied stove, it took a sense of humor, I suppose, not to consider the twenty-mile drive a futile effort.

His phrasing of sentences was often thoughtless and ridiculous. Some of the members were often shocked at his observations. I remember once he told of an incident at the school where he taught. A girl and boy had been caught kissing in the hall and the matron who had found them wanted both expelled.

Our little minister laughed, "Why I said no, we couldn't expel them. Miss —— was just mad because she wasn't being kissed herself." His psychology was probably sounder than he knew. Knowing the college later, and its people, I think the college probably would have expelled a boy and girl for kissing in the hall. Strange education that would close its eyes to nature!

The next minister was of a more common type. His grammar confused me as to the rules of grammar which I had been taught, and he often grew highly emotional in the pulpit. This confused me too. He was a medium-sized man with a head and face out of proportion to his body. His thick hair was curly and unruly and rose in a sort of mass above his face. I was continually sorry for him.

There were seven children in his family. Small, anemic-looking, poorly dressed, they sat in church and were forced to provide a model for the rest of us. Their clothes were always somehow skimpy looking, and hung dejectedly, as if the material needed starch to make it crisp. In short, they were unnatural-looking children. The joyousness, the vigor, the health that is the right of anything alive, was missing in them.

This minister's wife was a person hardly five feet tall, with bad coloring and zeal for the Christian work. She, too, was small, with a fervent, worried look in every glance. The family had not been at our church but a few months when she died. Another baby was on its way. The strain had proved too much for her.

So the family was left with the oldest girl of fourteen to look after the other six. She grew old overnight, the process having begun long before on every occasion when her mother was sick, which had been often. The minister had none too much money either, living in the small community he did, so the church decided on an old country custom of pounding him. What food each family could spare or give, we would take to the minister and his children. There are two things I remember about that singular event in my life. One was the overwhelming amount of food my father sent—a whole crate it took to hold the flour and staples he gave. "For," he said, "a man can't get along on just this canned stuff the people send." Then, on top of it all, he placed a tremendous watermelon, for it was summer. "That will give them a treat," he said.

I remember too the sense of brotherhood it gave me to see the people at the pounding. For I went along with the others, and watched the surprise on the minister's pleased face. When the first greetings were over, everyone stood awkwardly silent, embarrassed in the presence of their own generosity. Then someone started singing, and everyone followed. For all the solitary days I liked, there was also something good in this. This reaching out of a group to one, this sympathy made concrete. Surely it was a simple gathering and no one brilliant present, but it was more satisfying than many a tea and dinner I have been to since where the rule was cleverness and the fashion boredom.

More than all the people attached to the church, however, I recall the summer and winter Sundays of sitting on the walnut benches. The drone of insects in the air, the annoying buzzing of a fly around my head, the enervating languidness of summer mid-day. The deacon who was habitually sleepy sitting in his usual place, his head slowly drooping forward over his chest. The children sitting together, playing little hand-games with one another, drawing pictures on the Sunday School papers. And through the open window the red and green slope of the hill which ran up to the cemetery, the oak shade trees, and the mountains green and cool beyond.

During the winter, the little stove, with its long curved pipe going through the ceiling, was kept hot during the services until its sides glowed orange with the heat. Those who sat too close gradually loosened their coats while their faces turned red with the heat. Those who sat away from it suffered with chilly backs. My feet were always cold. Outside, the oak branches were all that was visible above the white-painted lower half of the windows. The leaves still clung to the branches, and tossed about in the strong winds and rains that came.

And always there was the singing. The sole instrument of music was the piano—and the human voice. Each vied to outdo the other. For these people sang about what they believed, and singing in the group was an outlet for whatever music they might have stored up inside of themselves. They sang rhythmically, paying less attention to the words and meaning than to the vowels, which they prolonged with gusto. Many of the songs I did not like—those which pictured the world as a vale of woe and tears, as something merely to be gotten through so that we could go on to heaven. The idea of heaven helped them go through everyday, but how much of heaven did they miss right in their own little gardens.

> Amazing grace, how sweet the sound,
> That saved a wretch like me,
> I once was lost but now am found,
> Was blind but now I see.

I wonder if they did.

UPON ONE WALL of our house, near the fireplace and above one of the walnut stands my father made, hung an Indian axe. It might have been called better a tomahawk, but I always heard it referred to as an axe. It was about a foot long and some ten inches wide, and was almost perfectly shaped.

For years I remember being impressed by this stone. Its cold gray surface and heavy resistance against the wire which bound it to the wall interested me. They suggested ruggedness and a formidable strength. Having the axe on our wall was like a constant reminder of the transiency of race and person, and an immediate memory of what sins our people had committed in the past against the people who had owned this country. Perhaps I should have gone all through grammar school believing that the Indian race was nothing more than a group of vandals who had, from their beginning, encroached on property intended to be the white man's from the beginning of time; that the Arapahoes and Sioux and Creeks were nothing more than fighters who had only awaited the coming of our race before they should commence their orgy of slaughter and scalping; I say, I should probably have believed this all through my first important years of school, had it not been for my father and mother. My father had always been interested in the study of the Indian tribes. There was some freedom and simplicity and harmony with nature about the Indians that he could appreciate. So I read some of the books he read, heard him discuss with Mother the origins and patterns of the Indian rugs we had on our floor, heard Mother tell of the arrowheads she and Daddy had found at various times about the place, and so I thought of the Indian as a designer, a craftsman, as well as a fighter who could defend his life if need be. Mother had several pottery vases of Indian origin which had come from the west, and she told me that the patterns used there were a story, had some symbolic meaning behind them, and so I always looked at those vases with a curiosity I did not feel for the little pictures on our other vases; the one was a language, with meaning and message, while the other was simply a piece of pretty decoration. The same held true with our rugs, and I can remember now how I used to sit, while Mother was reading or someone was talking in the room, and study the design on one rug in particular. There were two figures, as of turtles, woven into the picture, and one was made slightly thinner than the other. This always puzzled me and was a sort of secret I had with myself. Was the difference there because some Indian weaver had made a mistake with the wool, or was it there because of some special significance? I would not have found out if I could, for that was one of those inconsequential little problems a person likes to ponder when he sits before the fire and studies the object of his attention with drowsiness and a large, latent curiosity.

One day my father said to me, "Since you've been studying about the Indians so much, how would you like to have a bow and arrow?"

I was excited. I wanted one very much, all in a moment. I told him so.

"Well," he said, "if you want one so badly, how'd you like to make one?"

That would be even better. I was consumed with desire for a bow and arrow.

When we started the process that day, I did not realize how long it would take, or how long it would be before I would have arrows spinning straight and strong. First, there was the wood to get for the bow. That was the most important thing, my father said. The wood had to be right, and it had to be cured. We went out into the woods, he with his "light axe," which meant this was not the heavier axe he kept for wood-chopping. He chose a young ash tree for the bow. Standing so slim and long, it seemed a shame to cut this young thing for a mere plaything which I should use.

"It will be alright," Daddy said. "There are others near and they will replant seeds to take this tree's place. Besides, the woods just here are too thick for their own good."

We cut the young sapling and took it home.

"Ash will be good because it is elastic and will bend well," he said. "The ash here is not as good as some of the ash trees in other parts of the country. But it will do and make you a good arrow as long as you will need it."

The wood cured interminably, or so it seemed to me, and was half-forgotten for awhile. Then we finished making the bow one day. The wood was light and limber, and how carefully he made the notches one in each end, where the string could wind and hold the bow bent stiff. He talked to me as he worked, his pipe clenched between his teeth as usual, giving a peculiarly restrained manner to his speech.

"Now this side of the bow, where the string goes, is called the belly of the bow. The other side is called the back. You can find bows of different length; most of the good ones are six feet long. But since you are little and cannot pull as hard at first, I have made this only five feet, but it will be good all the same."

It was. I helped him tie the cord, and I recall how his knee bent forward slowly as the peeled, narrow length of ashwood bent slowly back under his pressure. When he had found the curvature that satisfied him, he held the wood still against his knee and I gave him the end of the cord which he had fastened already at the opposite end. Carefully he looped the string, and drew it taut between the bow ends. Then he fixed the knot, cut the spare ends and my bow was completed.

My lesson in shooting the arrow was of the feel of wood curving against one hand and the drawn quivering of the arrow in the other as it poised ready to be loosed against the air. I learned what a steady eye and keen focus meant, and where to aim and how. When finally I did know how to arch my arrow in the air, what a thrill it was to feel it sent out into space and watch it go lightly, slicing through the space toward a tree or marker. Again, to send it straight up, shooting toward the clouds, as if to spear a stray wisp and bring it back to earth. Limply, with relaxation, the arrow would fall to the ground again, landing easily, feathered side up.

It is such little commonplaces as these, brought forth and executed at the right time, that educate a child—or man. Through making, using, feeling some object which the Indian had made and used, however unlike were details of the two kinds of bows and arrows. I knew a closer kinship with him. Through touching the ashwood as he might have touched it, and shooting an arrow with the same taut string that he knew, how much more I could understand many other phases of his life or character which would seem at first unrelated to this. I had not only read from books about the Indians—I had seen their designs, felt their pottery, and helped make a bow as they might have made. Now I would not doubt that this was a race of people made for other things than war and massacre; the wind, the clay, the language of the woods was theirs.

Where I walk to school each day
Indian children used to play . . .

I do not know the rest of the poem, but shall I ever forget the wonder of repeating those two lines to myself when I first learned them in primary school. They were gone, all the feet which might have walked where mine were now. I would never know the people they carried. At best, however, I could attempt to understand them.

IN MY AUNT MAUDE's apple trees, there appeared this spring a novelty my two little cousins and I could not figure out at first. In the beginning we noticed it in a large old winesap tree, and it took the form of a web-like mass which filled a crotch between two limbs near the top. The web was grayish in color and seemed filled with some sort of bug caught in its meshes, or something not yet alive. We poked at it a little and forgot about it. Then we found other such webs in other trees and told Aunt Maude about them. She came to look. "Lord, some kind of caterpillar or pest, I guess, that will ruin my apples this year."

They had even wound their web around the horseshoe, which she had hung in one of the trees for luck, until it was hardly visible. She was forced to laugh at the comedy of the thing.

They were indeed caterpillars. Tent caterpillars was the whole name for them, and they were most harmful to apple trees. My aunt asked an old neighbor man about them.

"Caterpillar nests in apple trees? Law yes, many's the time I seen 'em." He stood on her porch and looked out over the trees. "Why, I remember years ago there come a reg'lar plague of 'em. They'd hatch out and start eatin' on a tree till they wa'nt nothin' left on it. Law, I remember once as how a man said to stand in his front yard and look toward his apple trees, you wouldn't think there was ary green leaf or bud on it. But when you walked out and looked—why, sure enough there wa'nt." He paused a minute chuckling at the wit of his little story. Then, with foreboding he went on, "Now, that's what they can do alright—strip an apple tree cleaner'n the inside of a whistle. I'd do somethin' about those trees, Miz Maude. Law, I would."

"Well, he was cheerful about it anyway," Aunt Maude laughed when he was gone. "But it's the truth that all I have is bad luck around this place."

Now we looked at the caterpillar nests with increased interest. Soon we could see the moving squirming worms themselves inside that glue-like covering which surrounded two or three hundred of them at a time. It would not be long until they would hatch, when they had eaten up the nourishment in the substance which surrounded them. Then they would go out on their own, crawling along the limbs and trunk of the tree, to eat hungrily, as the old man had said, on whatever green stuff they could find.

We decided to burn the nests. We took long sticks, tied cloth around the ends, dipped them in kerosene and held them under the nests. It was a loathsome job—I am sure that was all it was to my aunt—but in a way, it was fascinating too. That wriggling, twisting mass of elemental life hardly fresh from the egg was unforgettable. It was like the whole mass of life on this planet must have looked before order came about.

I stood there at the trees, watching the worms fall to the ground and begin to crawl in every direction, seeing the bright blue-orange flame leap up through the branches of the tree, until at last there was a clean place in the crotch of the limbs—and I was as held by the writhing worms, though it almost made me sick to watch so many, as a little bird can seemingly be charmed before a snake. We three children found something repulsive and fascinating at the same time in those egg and worm masses. Even in the repulsion there was something which touched our imaginations. It was so biologically true, I think, that we could not help but study it.

The next day we went out to the orchard and felt the apple buds to be safe in the unmolested trees. The only signs of the evening before were a few darkened places on the bark where our flames had touched, and the disturbed ground under the trees where we had trampled the worms into the earth.

Besides, they would have their vengeance soon enough.

twelve

···

THE BEGINNING of the year I was twelve, Daddy was forced to bed with a violent attack of rheumatism. It was the first time in his life he had ever spent a day and night consecutively in bed. If he had known at the beginning of the illness that he was to be confined for considerably more than a month, I wonder what reaction he would have made! But it is a wise provision that we are not permitted to see from one moment to the next what will take place, and so we are permitted to hope at every turn of the wheel. Mother and I hoped each day, too, with him, and believed that with the next day, or the next week, he would be on his feet again. I hated to see him in the bed. It was so unnatural for him, made him seem so out of his natural element, that every day when I came home from school I wished that I might find him sitting downstairs.

It is a hard thing to watch anyone in pain, too, and for a child the impressions seem even more vivid than for an adult. I could not help but watch my father when he was in pain, and I spent all the energy I could in running errands for him, fetching this or that, in hopes I suppose, that with enough of my care and labor, he would recover. It must have been this activity which led him to say to me one day,

"You don't save enough of your energy, little girl." (He still called me little girl in spite of the fact I had begun to believe I was outgrowing his endearment.) "You run up the steps when you might walk, you use your hands when you might simply stand still. You won't be a great person until you've learned to handle your energy—use it without it using you." (I suppose I had told him before this some of my aspiration to become a "great" person, the usual dreams of twelve years old.)

I don't believe his advice wrought the transformation he might have hoped for. Does any advice, ever, I wonder? But certainly it stuck with me, and perhaps unconsciously has influenced some of the excessive energies I may have been prone to spend from time to time.

We came to know each other a good deal more during this illness, for when I sat in the bedroom with him in the evening, or Mother and I went upstairs to do our reading or sewing, the air seemed to be ripe for conversation. One of those times I know that I had been assigned to write a paper in school on what I wanted to be when I grew older. I had decided I wanted to be a poet, having written an ode to a churn, a parody on Kipling's "L'Envoi," and similar evidences of talent.

"Well, I shouldn't think it would be so hard for you to write," my father said slowly, holding his twisted hands before him and studying them carefully. "It's according to what you're going to write. Well, it won't be so hard to tell about all the shiny, attention-getting things people notice or want, as it will be just to settle down and live, and then try to tell about that."

But perhaps I make him sound too much like the oracle. How far from the truth then, for most of the time we laughed and talked and discussed those things that are so simple a child doesn't remember what was said or done, but simply remembers the atmosphere and mood that permeated the room. Those are the times one cannot put quotation marks around and capture on paper, for it is the very tenuousness of their nature, the very subtlety of their tone that makes them sweet.

To have visited as little as we ever did, and to have known as few people as my father apparently did, it still surprises me when I recall the numbers of people who came to call on him during that January and February. They came on Sundays and through the week, they asked about him and left, or they went in and talked with him and stayed so long we had to ask them to leave in order that he might rest. They were so different and so varied that their comings and goings form a very matrix for the days of his illness. There were friends from the valley, members of the church, friends from town, and people who had worked with him on our place. The Banks's came, the girls and their brother, and stood uncomfortable before him lying in the bed and in the strangeness of the room. All of these people talked to him and enjoyed their visit, and yet there was an aloofness about his nature which did not permit him to follow the patter of their conversation. He would not repeat for them the triteness of their own little platitudes which permitted them to believe that they had thought about the problems of life and solved those problems for themselves. He would not agree with them and he would not tell them the things that they wanted to hear; and yet there was about his aloofness a kindliness, there was about his ways—which they considered eccentric—a respect, that made people feel the honesty of what he said and thought. And the kindliness and the respect drew them to him, where otherwise they would have been angered and humiliated by his difference from themselves.

I found much joy in the increased visiting list to our house, and even made a list of those who came to call each day. It was not long, however, before I began to know what it was that Mother and Daddy had meant in their preference for solitude over the constant comings and goings of people. Excitement had begun to take the place of quieter enjoyments, and I began to realize there was a difference in excitement and in happiness. The two were not synonymous. I believe there are a great many people who yet do not realize that.

If my father had read before his sickness, now he went beyond any previous amount and read almost constantly. History was one of his favorite reading subjects, and many times when I came home from school I would find him reading in some thick book upon almost the identical phases of history which we were studying in class. His appetite for history meant a great deal to me. It gave me something which I never found at school; that was a sense of what history really was—the romance, the wonder behind each page of its story. He would read to me about the Revolution, about the Civil War, and add to what he read the knowledge which he remembered from other books or essays. He would tell me about the men of a certain period and what they did—what they invented, what they discovered, how they fought or how they lived, and in the telling of it he would make the events and periods come alive, come so alive that they had meaning which carried over to that very moment when he was sitting in the bed telling me about it. We had a small brown book I recall, which was named *Fifteen Decisive Battles*. From the Persians and the Greeks through Waterloo, it told of the major battles which had turned some tide of history. When my father gave me that book to read and use as source material for an essay I was to write, I caught a glimpse of the struggles of men down through the centuries. Struggles for power, land, religion, freedom, and always, above the generals and the emperors, the horde of common people who carried the burdens and after all decided the matters in the end. Yes, my father made those fifteen decisive battles decisive for me.

> The mountains look on Marathon
> And Marathon looks on the sea,
> And musing there an hour alone,
> I dreamed that Greece might still be free ...

When he spoke those lines with all the feeling and rhythm inherent in them, I might have stood myself, looking on Marathon and dreaming. Suddenly I felt that there was no battle ever fought, no victory ever won, but that its waves of influence had washed over the years and made the present as it was.

My father enjoyed biography too. I think it is almost a rule that as people grow older they become more interested in reading biography than when they are younger. These, too, my father discussed, telling my mother and me incidents he had read in the books, chuckling over humorous parts, enlarging on the serious aspects. We brought our reading into our lives and made it a real aspect of our day's activities. What we found in a book wasn't something to be stored away and dusted off every few years when the time to display our knowledge came around. Rather it was something to be used in carrying on our own affairs, enlarging our ideas and our imaginations. Financiers, writers, naturalists, emperors, and presidents—anyone's biography was welcome. He read them carefully and thoroughly, taking them into himself and endowing them with meaning and with purpose.

Then there was always Horace Kephart's woodcraft book, collections of poetry, and the tales of Sherlock Holmes—which never lost their interest for me. And why would they, when I had reading with me a tall lean man who smoked a pipe as well as Holmes, and who was as interested in the story as I? In reading a book aloud, a great deal counts on the person who is with you at the reading.

In February the doctor began giving my father injections in the vein. I shall never forget watching that first injection. My mother had gone out of the room, but there was something which held me spellbound as if I had to watch what went on. The doctor wrapped the tube around Daddy's arm above the elbow, and faintly below one could see the blue vein which stood so near under the skin. The needle seemed inches long as he held it to the light, and quickly, before I could turn away he plunged it into the vein. Miraculous medicine, which can flow from a clear glass bottle into our blood and through our body, healing us, creating health within us! The sight of that sickening thrust of the needle had gripped my stomach, and now I walked away. What in me had rebelled so at the sight, had made my very knees watery beneath me. Yet the realization of the small miracle which was going on at that very moment, as the colorless fluid poured slowly from the bottle through my father's blood, was no less unforgettable.

At last spring came, and my father began to grow better. Then one day I came from school, and as I walked down the driveway Mother called me to the side of the house where she was working in some flowers. She pointed toward the upper window. There in the open window sat Daddy, his nightshirt white and clear against the sunshine. What happiness there is in the recovery of someone you love!

In the pond below the lawn, the bullfrogs had begun to croak, their guttural cries filling the air with a final farewell to winter. The ground where Mother was digging smelled cold and fresh, and at the edge of the garden the iris bulbs had sprouted several spears of green. And up in the window above us sat Daddy, breathing in the newness which is almost too sweet, too stirring.

"It's spring," he called, and I shouted back.

EVERYTHING IN NATURE follows a routine. There is a rhythm of night and day, birth and death, eating, breathing, and sleeping, which is so implacable, so inherent in the very essence of being, that we seldom if ever realize its presence or the strength of its force upon us. It is a rhythm so strong that we are caught in its current the moment we are born—even before we are born, from the moment we are conceived—and are carried along on its momentum until we die. At the same time, its force is so inevitable, so all-enveloping, that we can disclaim its presence and argue about our freedom at the very moment we are playing our role in the pattern and routine planned and designated since the beginning of time. For no living thing is ever free. From the amoeba and the paramecium to man himself, he is always bound by the law of species and always compelled by the necessities of natural existence to move within a certain range and follow a special pattern of activity.

The one great freedom he *can* possess is freedom from his fellow man. That is why the person who lives with nature is and can be the only really free person. In Nature he is compelled only by those laws so primal and universal that they govern the lives of plant and planet and rock as well as his own little existence. At least in Nature there are no man-concocted statutes which must be considered and weighed until the mind has forgotten all else but the pondering of those faulty human rules. And who will watch the nesting of catbirds and cardinals in the spring, who will sense the rise of sap in the grapevines and cherries and maples, who will feel the warmth of noon sun and the coolness of night on his skin, and not realize himself the magnificent part of some incomprehensible yet real and believable rhythm of existence?

My father and mother were great believers in routine. They followed the revolving cycle of the seasons and became, through their planting and harvesting, a part of that cycle. How many times when I was small can I remember Mother saying, on some yet cold and misty day,

"There's spring and planting in the air. I'll buy some seed today."

And sure enough, when a few days had passed, there would be the ground, still cold and dark looking, but unmistakably throbbing with new-found fertility.

How beautiful were the stores where we went to buy our seeds each year. What an event it was, this simple buying of latent life. First, there was the smell. It was the dry, dusty, various odor of barrels filled with spring seed. There was mixed in with this the damp fresh smell of the square watered boxes where tomatoes and cabbage and other plants were growing thick and green. While Mother and Daddy stood pricing and buying, I would go to the great barrels full and brimming with grain, and let handfuls run between my fingers. Both hands I would take and scoop them high with seeds, then watch the thin fine stream they made falling back where they came from, slipping through my hands with a smooth soft feel. Sometimes, when no one was looking, I would plunge one arm into the barrel, down down through the cool smooth seeds which gave way on either side to the pressure of my arm and flowed up higher around the edges of the barrel in which it stood. There, in some dark dusty corner of the cobwebby seed store I would stand and my hand would rest, deep and cool in the heart of all this fertility which might before long become a wide field of rye or oats or clover, bending to the wind, rising to the sun.

The small packages of seeds were no less fascinating. Outside, on the paper cover, would be drawn a brightly colored specimen of what the seed inside was to produce. And always how lusciously red was the meat of the big Ponderosa tomato, how tender and green were the curling leaves of the early lettuce and spinach, how golden and ripe with milk was the Golden Bantam corn.

Then came the turning of ground, the smoothing of dirt, the laying off of rows. My father did not plow—it was the one thing he gave in to because of his heart, and besides we were without a horse or plow and had insufficient work to merit either. But the rest he did, laying the rows with never a guide and getting them right and straight as a poplar grows. With a length of chain dragging from his hands behind him, he would walk across the plowed ground, back and forth, leaving behind him a series of straight long lines where rows would be.

When sowing the seeds, he and Mother would divide the packages—one to broadcast the spinach and rape and mustard in the green bed, to drop the yellowed peas, and carrot and beet seed; the other to plant the lettuce and radishes and onions, and maybe early corn. Watching them, I vaguely realized then the hope and belief it took to plant a garden. Sowing seed is a great act of faith. It takes faith to believe in the miracle that out of tiny brown seeds will spring rows and rows of healthy plants and vegetables. It is faith in the natural forces of sun and water and all the chemistry that lies within the soil. And it is faith in some great force which rises preeminent behind all Nature.

Twelve

So my father and mother followed the cycle of the seasons. They were at home in the world. At home because, ironically enough, they had found their true being outside of what is usually named the world. Their spirits drank from clear deep wells as intangible and real as the force of the rhythms they lived by, and followed their examples of order as naturally as any child of nature would. It was a rhythm like the caesuras and cadences of poetry, not the short pattering iambs and dactyls of verse.

But this perhaps sounds grand and other-worldish. It simply meant that in everyday terms the chickens were fed at seven in the morning, and our cows were milked at five o'clock in the afternoon. We ate at seven-thirty, twelve-thirty and six, and we were as careful with the regular eating of any life about us as with our own. It was a habit of getting up and lying down, carrying on our biological functions with a rhythm of existence and a pattern of activity that corresponded to the life around us and made us harmonious with it. I do not believe anyone can do his work as it was meant to be done, or find the happiness he was meant to find, if he lives without this rhythm which we see profound about us in every moment of natural life.

But it is the way of all children as they grow older, vaguely to wish for another kind of life. As I saw more how other people lived, and as I began to grow more sophisticated, or thought I was, this regularity grew irksome to me. I wanted to eat at odd times, late in the night, as Catherine's family did. I wanted to go to bed later and get up at different times, as Evelyn's family did.

"When you eat early and regularly, think what a good long evening you have ahead to read or walk in," my father said.

"If you miss the early morning, you miss the best time of the day," he said again, "and it's not like any other time."

But I persisted in my waywardness, and since then, many times, I ate at odd hours and rose at my leisure and found but a skeleton of any routine in my living.

I do not believe I have ever been so in tune with the infinitesimal of life, or found more happiness in the nuances which surround every brief example of nature, than in those years when I was young and rhythm was as natural as the air we breathed and a part of every breath.

I KNOW now that every place does not have a Milligan Hollow. However, there was a time when I thought a Milligan Hollow was as natural a part of a home as a yard, or steps or a porch. I spoke of it as one speaks of the living room or kitchen.

"I went up in the Milligan Hollow to find that lady slipper," I would say to some curious visitor, and could neither understand nor find reason for explanation in the fact that she did not seem to be familiar with this spot.

Gradually it dawned on me (perhaps I was a slow child) that this spot was peculiar to our own place; that it was the name of the ravine which had been found behind our own particular house and that no one outside the family could possibly know where or what it was.

So I will tell you.

It was a beautiful little ravine. It lay between a mountain and the hill that was directly behind our home. It was deep with rather sharp sides, and at the bottom flowed a stream which came from the spring at the head of the hollow. When we had moved to the place, my father had built a reservoir at the spring, and this was where our water came from. The overflow still made a stream through the ravine, however. There were trees and woodland on one side and a cleared pasture on the other. In the pasture part I found violets in the spring, and on the woodland side I found laurel and lady slippers, those mountaineer relatives of the orchid family. At the very head of the ravine and just below the spring were old apple trees, several of them. They were twisted, overgrown, uncared-for trees, and yet during some years they showered apples on the ground, large red spicy apples. I never knew the name for them. We would walk up in the fall and find them covering the ground, some split open because they hit the rocks, others bruised or torn by their fall to the ground. It was strange that apple trees should have been here anywhere, in the midst of poplar, black walnut, maple, oak. It gave a curious sensation to run across this cultivated species of tree in the midst of natural unplanted trees. Even though they had been uncared for for years, there was still an air of difference about them.

This was the story of the hollow, as far as I could ever learn. Its story gave the place a great background of interest for me. It was a memento of another of those lonely old souls who wander the earth for peace and a place to call their own.

His name was Milligan. The mountain people called him Old Man Milligan. He had come from Scotland and his accent was thick and strange to the people around. This was one of the first barriers to his communicating with them. Then he built himself a cabin back in this cove, which was then lonely and a good distance from any other house. He owned a dog, and hunted, walked, or just sat, as he pleased. The cabin was small, but enough for one man. The hollow which stretched below his cabin was small, too, and narrow. The mountains around protected him from wind in the winter and too bright sun in the summer. The seasons came and went with him in the midst of them—spring flowering up to his very doorsill, and the winter snow making a silent hidden earth around him. What he did, what he thought, as he sat in his little cabin and ate his food, or looked out the door to the trees and little stream beyond— why, who can tell? Perhaps great, profound thoughts; perhaps nothing.

The people were suspicious of him. He did not talk much; when he did he used queer expressions, expressions they had never heard before. One night one of the children of a valley family came home and said he had been to Old Man Milligan's.

"He was eating a possum," the little boy said. "I ate some too."

They did not eat possum, these people who lived in the valley. They did not approve of the mountain people who did eat it. They were shocked. "Don't go back again," they said to the boy. "He's a dirty old man," they said to one another.

Twelve

....

146

He was not a large man; his beard and hair grew longer than most, yet he cut both himself, and looked after his own needs, calling on no one.

Sometimes he would talk with some of the men he chanced to meet on the mountains, or along the road. He talked of hunting with them. "I caught a raccoon the night before last," he said to one, rolling his r's in the rich accent of Scotland. "Do you know I had to cut a tree to get it, too? A fine big chestnut tree it was—a regular belly-stretcher."

It was expressions like that that the men were not accustomed to. "He's a funny ol' feller," they would say, "but queer too, somehow 'r nother."

I don't know how many years Old Man Milligan lived in the hollow there. He planted apple trees in front of his cabin and drank the water from the ever-flowing spring behind. Something, some place, some person, some event, some whim, called him away. He left the apple trees behind, for us to eat their apples, and scarcely dreamed that years later the story of his years there would stir the fancy of a child who lived nearby his place, in something of loneliness too.

No doubt he was a dirty, shiftless fellow who had wandered to the mountains and chose to live there in peace awhile. His cabin would probably have been a makeshift thing which let in cold in winter and was never clean in the summer. But what can we not create from stories of people we have never seen, and places we have never known? While we are dreaming, let us dream, and give the material world the back-seat for a moment.

THERE IS for children a fascination in everything alive. Later, when adult fears and superstitions have been implanted in their minds, their curiosity and trust are dulled. But before that time, a hornet's nest, a mud-dauber's home, an ant hill, are all as exciting as any adult-written fairy tale or adventure book. At least, they were for me. The whole insect world was a mystery, and perhaps more interesting than the "pretty" flowers.

The first time I ever saw a hornet's nest I could not believe that it was built by those tiny flying wasps. It hung under an eave of my father's workshop and had grown to sizable proportions before we found it. The grey papery mass was perfectly shaped, and it was difficult to believe that its proportions had been wrought by instinct alone.

Perhaps the mountain people recognize something of the feat these hornets accomplish, for often on the porch and sometimes in the front room of their cabins, you will find one of these nests. Usually it is unique in some respect, perhaps by size or placement on some fork or limb. But it is there before them as an example of what the insect world can do.

"These hornets manufactured paper before any of our machines were even dreamed of," my father told me.

"How?" I wanted to know.

"By taking bits of wood, pieces of bark that have flaked off planks or posts, and chewing these particles in their mouth. Processing would be the industrial term, I guess. Then they add these gradually to the nest until it grows and grows, suiting the size of the family it must hold inside."

"But how do they get it so round?" I demanded.

"*That* is the secret," my father answered.

I wondered about the wind and the rain, why it could not tear down in a moment anything so fragile looking as this nest. But I figured that maybe that was also a part of the secret, to make the nest stronger than it would appear.

Then there were yellow-jacket nests too. They were not so large or intricate as the hornet nests, and built in better protected places than the hornets. Usually there was only a single layer of the comb, where in the larger hornet nests there were layers upon layers of these combs. We were never quite so afraid of the yellow jackets as the hornets, either. They seemed a little more reasonable, but the hornets were nearly always angry, or sounded so at least.

Akin to these, and also in the wasp family, yet much different, was what I called the dirt-daubers. I found some of their mud cells on the sides of an old deserted house one day, and was curious to know what had built these strange-looking formations. They might have belonged to the adobe tribes of the insect world. Seeing that they looked crumbly and dry, I took a stick and tried to gently dislodge one from the wall so that I might take it home with me and find out what it was. But I was mistaken. That mud was hard and tight as brick, and would only chip off when pried with hard strong jabs of my stick. I decided to leave them where they had been intended. There were no holes at the ends of the tubular structures. They looked like little pipe organs with no places for the music to come out. The structures themselves varied in length. I wondered what they were for. So I picked up my stick again and seeing that there were so many of the clay tubes hanging along the walls and ceilings, I decided to sacrifice this one to my exploration. After I had pried a little while, I came to a tiny cell near the opening of the tube, and in it was a dead spider. There were other similar insects in other cells along the tube.

When I reached home, my father told me the name of the insect which had built these mud nests. "They're called mud-daubers," he said, "and the spiders that you found were to feed the young mud-dauber in that nest when it hatches." He told me too that a mud-dauber lays its egg in the last of these cells, and leaves with the egg enough food, in the form of other insects, to keep it alive until it can fare for itself in the world. Then it emerges into the day; having feasted on its prearranged supply of food it is now forced to find its own.

Ants, of course, are probably the most fascinating single insect in the world. I remember sitting on warm days and watching the goings and comings of the inhabitants of many an ant hill. How busy they always seemed, how intent on doing their job. And what was most amazing, they always seemed to know their job so well. No hesitation, no questioning, just doing their work. The little beads of sand which usually stood outside the hills were piled in a neat cone-shape around the entrance. Sometimes I would rake bits of that dirt over the entrance, and for a moment there would be obliteration of the hole. Then, indomitable, the ants would struggle through, re-piling the disturbed sand where it belonged. Or again, I would sometimes put a grass or small stick in a path I had watched an ant go over several times. Always she would go up and over and down the grass, up and over and down the stick, side-stepping nothing but treading relentlessly on toward her goal. Once in awhile I would see a black ant and a red ant meet, those two large species which are each good fighters. After this, I read about the habits of the ants, and found that their battles are as scientific and as momentous as are human battles—at least to the ants. For in the case of the black ants, it means whether or not they will die and whether or not their pupae, from which are yet to hatch the baby ants, will be captured by the enemy. And in the case of the red ants it means that they must capture these pupae of the enemy so that the young black ants can become their slaves; for the red ants are so highly developed in their weapons of warfare that they cannot feed themselves, and must die without these slaves. Strange, unbelievable world which goes on at our very feet and so remarkably resembles our own world as to give us pause a moment.

Then there were the insects which filled the summer and early fall nights with sound. By rubbing their wings, by vibrating the covers of those wings, by various nature-given ways and means, they made the summers unlike any other seasons of the year. I would lie in bed at night, four large windows open in an even larger room; one looking toward the hillside behind our house, two opening above the garden, and the other open toward the creek and the meadow beyond. Here was sound all around me, a hundred voices shouting a language which, if I but understood it, might tell me many curious things.

Last of all these night criers to come was the katydid. "Six weeks till frost," my mother said, the first night we heard its song in the air. So there was always something sad about its chirping, pleasant and steady though it was. It came with the days of the goldenrod and the dusty purple asters along the road, and with their going, it went too. "Katy-did, Katy-didn't . . . Katy-did, Katy-didn't . . ." I could lie and follow the songs of the little green insects scattered through the trees and grasses, and finally fall asleep, hearing the voice of nature all about me.

ONE OF THE MEN in our community who was generally respected and of whom many stood in awe was an old widower who supposedly was well-to-do financially. I heard people mention his name. Mother sometimes remarked to my father that she had seen him at church that Sunday, but I did not know him at all except by sight.

He was a heavy-set man with a broad face, wrinkled skin, graying hair, and enigmatical blue eyes under bushy brows. His hands were broad, too, with short stubby fingers and soiled fingernails. When he stood talking with other men he seemed to enjoy being the authoritative frog in the puddle, and he would speak to them in the thoughtful manner of a successful man imparting some of his secrets to a group of novices.

One day my father ordered some wood for our fireplace from him. He owned several farms and pieces of woodland and sold whatever he could off of either. We expected the wood next day but it did not come. Then late that night, long after darkness had fallen and we had settled for the evening, a ring of the bell, and there stood a wide-eyed negro man. It was winter and the snow which had begun that noon was sticking to the ground, making it wet and muddy. The wind was fairly high and made the cold more piercing than it otherwise would have been. The man was shivering.

"I brought your wood, mistah," he said.

My father looked at him and at the snow. "On a night like this, at this time of night?" he asked.

"Yes suh," was the negro's answer. "I done thought I'se all through fo' the day an' jes' as I'se gettin' ready to leave, Cap'n he come out and ast me would I jes run up here with this load of wood. It was some run," the man grinned, "what with snow and all."

"I should say," my father replied.

"An' then I got stuck a li'l piece off the pavement down here and had to unload pa't of the wood to make the wagon lighter. So if y'all 'll jes' show me where to put it, I'll be unloadin' what I done got."

"Just a minute, I'll show you," my father said, and came back to the hearth. He changed his shoes and put his slippers in the corner.

"Be careful helping him," my mother said. "Don't strain." She knew beforehand that he was going to help the negro standing out in the snow.

"I won't." My father looked at her. "Think of sending anybody out at that hour in this kind of a night."

Mother and I sat inside by the fire and listened to the noises of them unloading outside. The logs made soft thuds as they struck the ground, then rolled over to pile against the others. My father would be standing there piling the wood neatly, I knew. Then we heard the sound of the team as it went out the driveway, and as it returned a while later with the rest of the wood he had been forced to throw off down the road. More sounds of the wood being unloaded, then we heard my father's feet stomping the snow off his shoes on the porch. He opened the door and called to us, "We're coming in to warm."

Slowly, bashfully, the negro came in, cold yet afraid to avail himself of the heat.

"Come in," my father said. "Sit down and warm your feet. It's cold out there," and he rubbed his hands together. It was the most genial I had ever seen him. The man sat down in a corner chair uneasily, on the side of the cushion. My father and mother talked a little, then Daddy said, "You out this late at night often?"

"Yes *suh*," the man answered. "Cap'n he always givin' us niggers some li'l ol' job to do after we done through fo' the day. We don' say nothin' 'bout it though. We 'fraid he won't pay us a-tall fo' the day then."

"Have much trouble about your pay?"

"Naw suh, not so much. Co'se you see I borrows some money from Cap'n along. He jes' lets me pay it back a dime at a time. I borrows a dollah from him and he jes' let me pay a dime a week outa what I earn for a year, maybe a l'l more, and after awhile I got it all paid back. Yes suh, he's good 'bout loanin' us money, Cap'n is."

"Many of the other men owe him money?" Daddy asked.

"Most of us that works for him aroun' the fahms does. I don' reck'n they's ha'dly a one of us but owes him somethin'. But law's have mercy, they ain't ha'dly nobody aroun' but owes Cap'n somethin'—he owns jes' 'bout ever'thing." There was almost pride in the man's voice for the accomplishments of his employer. "An' I tell you, he ain't foolin' with none o' them people that lives in his houses down in the nigger part o' town. He don' get the rent, then out they goes. I done help him put a family out day fo' yestidday."

Suddenly he hushed, startled at the talking he had done. He shifted his big feet on the hearth where little puddles of melted snow had run off his shoes. My father did not speak. All at once he seemed tired.

The man muttered, "I reck'n I gotta go." He stood up, awkward in the large room and white light. For a moment he stood and looked around him as if he were in a daze. My father went to the door with him. "Thanks for bringing the wood," he said.

"Oh, that's awright," the man said and plunged off the porch, hurrying through the darkness toward his impatient mules.

We stood at the window and heard the wagon rattle across the boards on the bridge, listening until the sound of turning wheels had faded into the night.

"He didn't even thank you for sitting by the fire," I said.

"Why should he?" my father replied.

Twelve

....

153

We sat down in our accustomed chairs again. Daddy put on his slippers, Mother was finding her place in the book she had been reading. I had much to think about.

At last Daddy looked at Mother. "What kind of a life does a man like that lead?" he said.

ONE NIGHT during the summer I went to church, probably to hear some visiting minister speak. The windows of the church were open to the night, and any stirring wind that might find its way into the warm room. The large white lights glared from the ceiling, attracting all the insects and darting moths that are drawn by them into the strange rooms.

The voice in the pulpit was excited and rhythmic. It spread out over the benches of people and faded into nothingness. Now and then one of the men in the choir would brush his neck with an irritated sweep, ridding himself of one of the whirling little bugs which had strayed from the light for a moment. Some woman would fan a moth away from the baby which lay asleep on the seat beside her. If one of the boys caught a bug in his hand for a moment, there would be a flurry of giggling and movement along the seats where the boys sat together. These boys had come to church so that they could walk home in the darkness afterwards with one of the girls; the sermon was of little moment to them. But a bug . . . ah, a bug was different! It wasn't every day you had time enough to sit and watch a bug crawl around inside your fist.

I have not forgotten that night because there was a warmth and pleasantness to it, a heat that was soft and mixed with coolness. There was the feel of a crisp organdy dress, and watching the people as they sat and listened, or did not listen, all depending on what they had come for. Then, too, there was the moth, and that was a memorable thing.

It came drifting in through the front right-hand window, as if curious and yet unconcerned about this blaze of light. One of the girls who was sitting in the choir had helped me collect some of my butterflies. I saw her look at me quickly, and then turn back to the moth, so that she would not lose sight of it. It flew high at first, near the ceiling, cautious, circling the large light fixtures. I watched it, and out of the corner of my eye I could see her watching too. The moth was so large that several people had noticed it, and every once in awhile they looked up too, seeing the yellow shadow above them.

Then the real pantomime took place so quickly that I hardly knew what had happened. The moth had flown over the choir, gone to the lights, and again fallen lower, just above the heads of the people sitting there in their places. Swiftly, with no sound, I saw the girl reach her arm into the air, and leave an empty space where her hand had touched. She bent her head toward her lap now, and I could not make out what was happening, but I knew. She reached for an old quarterly which was lying on the bench in front of her, and I could tell when she pressed the moth quickly inside its pages. There was a silence about the whole action that gave it the curious quality of a pantomime. A little side-show acted out while the main performance took place in the pulpit, with the man's voice coming out like a rushing flood-filled creek.

After church, she came up to me on the porch, and handed me the quarterly. "I caught it for you," she said. How could I tell her that I had not wanted it, that although I had sought other moths, there had been something so free and graceful about this one that it would have been spared from me for the rest of its brief life?

It lay quite still on the paper—a beautiful Imperial moth. The soft yellow wings, with the old rose dusted across them, were motionless. There was a richness about the color and design that made the print of the Sunday School quarterly seem pale beside this Imperial splendor.

AN ECLIPSE of the sun is a great event for children. With me, it was an unbelievable phenomenon which puzzled me and brought up all sorts of disturbing questions. How far away was the sun, and how large was the sun compared to the earth? What happened when an eclipse came and how could anyone know when one was coming? Oh yes, there are innumerable answers the mind can seek when it is really begun on a field of questioning. And nowhere can the mind be made to feel smaller or more insignificant than when it tries to comprehend the functioning of the planets.

August the thirty-first the year I was twelve was the eclipse I remember so well. Mother and Daddy explained to me what would happen, and yet somehow I did not believe that darkness could come right in the middle of the afternoon. Somehow, the mind can seem to grasp a fact and yet have no actual comprehension of that fact at all. They told me if I would find some smoked glasses I could look at the sun perhaps, and watch the whole thing just as it happened.

School had begun the last of August, and so I was in school that day. Will I ever forget the preparations we made so that we might see the eclipse. The boys made small fires and held broken pieces of glass, which they had found around the grounds, in the heavy smoke they made by piling wet leaves on top of the flames. They smoked both sides dark, holding the glass gingerly so that none of the black would smear off on their hands and ruin their chances for seeing the eclipse. Then someone started the rumor that old negatives from Kodak and camera snapshots were fine to use, and we rushed to the houses which stood near the schoolgrounds, demanding from the irritated women who answered the door that they provide us with negatives. Some way, we did manage to get a handful, and these we carefully distributed among those friends who had done us favors in the past. With all the equipment we had scraped together, we were well prepared to watch anything that might happen.

At last the time came, and we all stood out in the schoolyard, the dust from the grounds billowing around our feet. Our glasses and negatives and hand-smoked pieces of glass were all focused on the sun. There we stood, a hundred or so of us, staring with wide eyes into the face of the sun, watching a phenomenon which took place out in the space beyond us. And we were young and eager and excited, and doubtless believed that the passage over the sun had been arranged for our own benefit, finding it incomprehensible that the earth might move without knowledge of us and that the planets beyond might exist without knowledge of the earth.

Slowly, the darkness came. "It was not a total eclipse, but pretty near," I wrote in my diary. And at the end, "That was about the only thing of much importance that happened today."

thirteen

....

ANYONE WHO STUDIES NATURE long in any form, or accepts the plants and animals as part of the world as real as himself, must come across the knowledge of the settling of America, and what took place during that settlement. When I came across the passages in the history books, which were merely hints of what had actually taken place, I wanted to know more about the gluttony which had ruled this country. My father gave me other books to read, and told me much himself, and during the telling much became clear. But it was unbelievable to me that in a hundred years and less, oh much less in some instances, the face of a country could be so changed, the character of a country be so altered. Somehow I had thought it was ages gone, hundreds of years ago, that the buffalo and the wild turkey and the tall trees had been common on the land. It had seemed so very long ago. But now, suddenly, I found that it was only a generation or so, only a few swift years, only yesterday, since these wild glories, so peculiar to the United States, had been demolished and despoiled in an unimaginable destructiveness.

In the zoo in the park on the other side of town, I had seen a buffalo. Its huge shoulders, lowered head, and skin, so different from other animals in the zoo, had interested me. I had watched it a long time as it stood, or walked so slowly, through the little sapling-planted plot of ground it had to call its own. How was my imagination then, to conceive of a day when there had been hundreds of thousands of these animals scattered over the plains in uncounted herds? More, how was I to believe that such numbers had existed so short a time ago? That was the hardest hurdle of all for my mind to make.

There had been buffaloes so plentiful that men felt no waste in killing one of the tremendous beasts to simply save the heart, or tongue, or hide. Others killed for sport, bringing down numbers of the animals to see them fall, to experience the thrill of the hunter. At first, the buffaloes were so plentiful that the killed were never missed. The plains could lie dotted black with the carcasses, and yet the numbers seemed undiminished. So the imaginations and the exploits grew, and there was no control over the man with the gun. For meat, for skins, for pleasure, and for sport, he waded into this sea of wild life and struck out blindly all about him. What fell and what remained was of little moment. There was only the present.

So the thundering feet were felled as they ran, and the bellowing voices were stilled as they protested, and the wandering symbol of America's wild life was exhausted.

There were the forests also. There were the oaks and pines and walnuts, the tall straight hardwoods, and all the woods which had never been touched by the hand of the white man before. The inconceivable awe and splendor of it, the untouched purity and aloofness, the unmatched virginity of this virgin timber. But did the eyes following the height from trunk to tip marvel in the beauty, or did they calculate the lengths of lumber such a tree would make? Did their eyes, wandering over hillsides and the lowlands covered with these forests pause to think the years behind this stand, or did they estimate what such a strip of land would grow if all the trees were burned off to the ground?

With unimaginable waste they slashed and cut and burned, and when they had cleared off all the land they wanted, they cut more timber for their houses; and when their houses were mostly built, they cut still other timber for their fires. And then the industries came which needed wood, and added the

Thirteen

demand which had been lessening. Down the swift-running rivers, between mountains and forests which still stood unmolested, floated the big logs. Thousands and thousands of them floating along the tie-drives, thousands and hundreds of thousands feeding the mouths of the sawmills. And sawmills over the country swarming like bees among blossoms, siding and slicing the lumber, spitting the heart out in sawdust.

Where were the tall trees now? Where was the shade, and the roots and the falling leaves? Instead were the barren hills and eroded fields; instead remained the dust and the heat and the flooding waters. Where he had cut, greed now reaped his harvest; where he had grown rich he now knew poverty. The tale was old, yet wondrously new to me. There was a patterned cycle at work somewhere; there was a Penalty for greed and curious justice coming to pass.

And the small game and the plants, what of them? Swept aside in the rush for something big, uprooted and killed in the passion for ownership which could let no living thing stay where it belonged but must needs take it into possession. The same remains today, and we see people every spring who must take the wild trillium and the lady slipper and plant it in alien soil where it will surely die. And the unique and disappearing sage hen, it is going from the prairies, leaving another empty place where something wild and beautiful had been.

These were the things my father told me about the history of our country in a hundred years and less. He himself had seen much of it take place, and this seemed to me, again, an inconceivable fact. So soon gone, so near to me, only in yesterday it had been, and now gone irrevocably. The buffalo and the timber and the untouched lives of living things—how many in the cities or in the ruined and washing countrysides can even picture to themselves what our country was or might have been, or could be? There is today to live and laissez-faire the watchword; or there is tomorrow and the remembrance of those who are to come.

Thirteen

THERE IS PROBABLY no more lonely sound on earth than the crying of dogs on the mountains in the night. A long stark cry it is, echoing through the gaps and down the ravines, echoing from a past when the dog was wolf and down through the centuries to its present stage.

During the fall, when the hunting reached its peak, we could hear the hounds almost every night, running along the hills. Sometimes their baying would be long and musical, with intervals between, but when the short sharp cries came, with eager rush and little space between, we knew the game was near, the scent still warm and strong from its running feet. I would wait with listening ears, wondering how the dogs must feel and look, their breath coming hard and fast into their lungs. And the wild thing, how was it? Were its eyes bright in the darkness, glowing in this last race between life and death, a race which must be run by all living things? Did its eyes dart into the crevices of rocks and stones along the way, did they measure the heights of the saplings where they might run? And finding no escape, did the pursued turn and face its pursuers, tasting something of pride and matchless abandon in the very position of its loneliness? I could follow the whole race in my mind, and depending on the barking, know who had won or lost.

As I say, to follow the cries of these hounds in the night was a lonesome experience. The trees stood ghost-like in the moonlight, their leaves silently falling around them; in the woods, the chestnuts would be falling with cushioned plops, and the wild grapes hung high and midnight blue, entangled in the branches of some dead tree. All the world around me was enfolded in beauty and in strangeness, and the embodiment of the strangeness and the beauty was in the voices of the hounds. There was nothing I could reach out and touch and have the sensations of the night explained, no vision which would carry me to the reality of the race. Yet I lay in my own bed, between crisp white sheets, and could feel the night come in around me.

Little wonder then that the music of the fox-race on the hills awakens like feelings in us, moving our memories through the unrealized passages of earth-remembrance into the dim corridors from whence we came. Surely we are from the past and breaths of all the nature we have sprung from are in us; so are we a part of men and women who lived in all the ages past, a link in some incredible chain which began in the foggy misty mornings of the world and will end in some long future twilight for the race of men.

ONCE WE HAD A ROOSTER that crowed in the middle of the night. Now a rooster that crows at night may not seem an odd thing to you, particularly if you have never owned chickens. But to us it was odd and disturbing.

This rooster did not crow at the beginning of the night, but began around midnight, and for an hour or two would give his cry which was meant to signal dawn. It was a startling cry the first night I heard it, and I sat up in my bed, certain that some animal was in the chicken house, perhaps after a hen or eating the laying mash from the trough in one corner of the hen-house. But all was silent. There was not even a wind to make noises among the leaves or branches, and the stillness seemed double-fold because the night was so completely dark. Then I heard him again, crowing with a voice that was foggy and sleepy in spite of all its alertness. I lay back in bed, warming my elbows under the cover, and shivered at the pleasantness of something at once familiar and peculiar. And lying there in the dark and silence, waiting only for this unnatural crowing, the quality of darkness seemed infinite and real to me. It was inescapable, it was unbearable. It was the night during which great owls came from their hollow trees and caught on the talons of their clawed feet the running mice and small bewildered birds. It was the night when dogs roamed over the mountains and followed the trails of rabbit and possum and fox, raccoon and bear. It was the night when unbelievable violences were done in the cities, and we would read about them the next morning in the newspapers. Night was the cloud under which men and animals prowled, hunting by their instincts and running through narrow canyons and down narrower alley-ways.

Again the sound of the rooster crowing came to me. It was a misplaced sound, this cock-a-doodle-do at midnight instead of morning. It stood as emblem of a whole pattern, an automatic part of which were the irreconcilable capabilities of a man's nature.

ONE OF THE MOST normal activities I ever undertook was a class in ballroom dancing. I had a great sense of rhythm for walking or skipping rope, but I had never been good at dancing. I had never tried any dancing, in fact, but I wanted to learn to waltz and round dance. I marvel now at just how much I did want to learn. Also, for various reasons I am surprised somewhat at my taking these lessons. But I did join a class and that is the point.

It was an average class. There were more girls than boys, one of the boys had exceptionally large and heavy feet, one of the boys was good-looking and a fine dancer. So it went. But the horror of facing those people for the first time. The horror of that first Saturday morning is something I cannot diminish, even now, in my mind. We lined up along the wall and our teacher gave us the box-step formula and we practiced the slide-draw, slide-draw routine. It was when we began the actual dancing that I was petrified. How calmly the others took the matter, how eagerly they waited for the music to begin, tapping their feet impatiently. What would I not have given on this earth to be like them then. They were all so alike, they were so ordinary, so beautifully terribly normal—what could I do in their midst but stare at them and wish with all my bitter heart that I was one of them.

These were the girls and boys who lived downtown; they rode the city buses home from school and paid six cents; I rode the country bus which was painted bright orange and carried all the mountain children. I could be at home with neither one. These were the girls and boys who rode bicycles, who had started even now to date one another, who had known already their first evening dress, first date, first dance. I was so far behind; there were so many things I must do for the first time still before me. I had walked in the woods and known the sound of the snow, seen the cycle of a tadpole's jellied mass becoming a frog, felt the rush and passage of the seasons—but these were suddenly discredited in my own eyes. I stood stripped of all that I had done, of all that I had ever wanted to do or been happy in learning, and what was left was pitiful and small. Before these girls who seemed so sophisticated to my inexperienced eyes, I stood helpless and incomparable. They could laugh and talk of nothing, they could make the right moves and place their hands so lightly on a shoulder; in short, they were so right. I was all wrong. The things I could talk of happily were not meant for snatched moments in a dancing class; where I knew to use my hands most beautifully and well was not around other people, but in the ground, around the house. I would have given half my heart to have been as those girls were to me then, the conquering, the lovely, the ordinary.

Then there was the boy. I do not know his full name now, but the given name was Paul. Paul was of medium height, his hair was brown, his eyes were blue, he was some four years older than any of the rest of us. He was in the dancing class to keep in practice. Since he was the only fair-looking boy in the class, naturally all the girls liked him. I determined to be different, not to like him, but I could not help myself. He was kind, his eyes were humorous, and he could make my steps come out right. But I? Ah, what was I like to him? I wondered then, I do now. I wonder if he knew, Paul, that he was the first boy I ever thought about, thought about when I was washing dishes or getting lessons; if he could ever imagine the bitterness I felt because I did not know his language, for I realized even then that I could not hope to know him. We were on either side of a chasm. We danced together once every week, for he had one dance with every student; the smell of his coat was grown-up and pungent; he spoke pleasantly and gently. But what was it I had missed? What, along the way, had I failed to understand, where had I been blind? Did he know then, or now, that it was him and his fellow dancers that I envied? I found peace and thoughtfulness and lost myself in the wonder of nature. That was my father's spirit in me. But where were the ones who could share my peace and thoughtfulness? I wanted the ordinariness of their laughter and their doings—I wanted to be one with them. I was very young and youth is not meant to be alone. That was my mother's spirit in me. Conflict without solution, staging such a battle that all of life must be a choice, one between the other, and always half regret that the undone was not done. Where the eventual answer lay, I could not tell, in people or in nature—but I know that for that moment of my life I would have pawned half my days of walking in the woods for an interval of dancing and meaningless chatter. Strange fate that leads us down a path, and while we know that ultimately our way is right, it makes fierce regret and bitterness in our heart that we could not know another path as well.

fourteen

THERE IS SOMETHING fine and beautiful in a child becoming aware of his body. That is, if the awareness comes naturally, as a culmination of a phase of his life which is over and done; if it comes slowly and develops as a realization of joy and of responsibility. So often, through a combination of unfortunate circumstances, the gradual beauty is destroyed. But seldom can the circumstances prove so strong that they prevent a great bounding joy from permeating unexpected minutes, or hours, of a child's life.

There used to be such flashes of happiness come over me that even to recall them now is something of happiness. From where, or why, or by what power they came, I do not know. But I suspect that it was the joy of youth, the exultation of bone and blood and flesh knitted together in an irreplaceable fashion. It was the beating of heart and the pounding of blood, the certainty of knowing that this was me and that in some matter and manner of genes and chromosomes I was something slightly different from any other living thing. It was the very slightness of difference that made the distinction sweet.

Especially I recall standing one afternoon on the hillside opposite our house, and for no apparent reason and from no apparent cause, the freshest elation I have ever known swept over me. It was exultation from the mind, but taking particular possession of the senses, so that to smell the air filled with only the slightest odor, or to feel the elasticity of the earth underneath the feet, was almost too good to take in all at once. What else but the searching, awakening senses of youth could be so highly strung, so finely taut? Since then in later years, I have seen boys, six or eight or ten, crowded into a rattletrap of a car and racing along the road under the moonlight, with unearthly yells and shrieks. They are the shrieks of youth, the cries of joy and energy and the beliefs which have met no disillusions. They have found the goodness of their own egos, the rapture of their own minds and bodies, and the harnesses of adult convention have not yet been slipped on them. So they race over the roads, into the country, into the city, and the world around them is magic, and the road is open before them. The heights and the depths are theirs, or so they believe. And this belief is their birthright and their rapture.

It was the same happiness as this, essentially, that came to me that afternoon.

Now I began to have an awareness of my body. I had come to the age of puberty, and my mother had explained to me the physique and functions of a woman. There was a whole new field of knowing opened to me; I wanted to be alone to think about the different focus life had come to have for me. Now I was not merely under the broad tabulation of a human; I was a member of a sex as well; my limitations became more real, my abilities more defined.

What is it to be a child, and suddenly stand on the entrance to that vague estate called adulthood? Every person would have a different tale to tell. For me, it was a combination of elements: a bit of physical pain, a little bitterness at leaving so suddenly a carefreeness and ignorance I knew would never exist again, but perhaps most of all a huge wonder at the makeup of the world. Everything seemed so planned, so foreordained, for even me who felt sometimes like the smallest cog in the whole machine.

Then there was the joy that I have spoken of. It was awakened, along with undreamed of emotions and ideas, and made intense by this new awareness of sex and function. It revelled in the stretch of arms and the feel of firm long legs beneath to walk and run and pivot in a whirligig of movement. It examined with eyes as new and bright as spring, the faintly traced curve of calf and thigh, the hopeful, barely discernible curves where breasts were born, and the sharply outlined sweep of back and neck. Perfection? What was perfection to those eyes? Neither the measurements of fashion nor the criteria of artists; simply, the mark of health and the resiliency of limbs. For every movement, every dance of youth, is a gesture of thanksgiving for the strength of bones and muscles and the right to live.

Plants and animals all around us are beautiful in the simple processes of their living. Why should it not be so with us? Surely I was closer to the heart of nature when I stood along her hillside that pulsing day than I have been since, for all the attempts made. That day I was not standing back and looking on at beauty. I was part of it. Such moments are possible only while self-consciousness remains unborn.

THE SUN SHONE a little brighter that morning my father came down the stairs. It was the first day of June, and with the going of May, spring had ended. Now the full-blown summer was here. The first tender peas from the garden, the first nasturtiums, the first flowering tree and bush on the hillside: all of these were in the past. The earth itself was a fraction closer to the sun, and in the spinning balanced order of days, warmth stretched like a magnet over the land, drawing forth the vines and leaves of seeds long planted.

During breakfast Mother said to him, "Your face is grey this morning."

The attack came about eleven in the morning. The sun was climbing toward noon, and the hazy buzzing sounds of June were loud in the clover field across the bridge. The pain of angina pectoris is acute, as any doctor will tell you. To watch it slowly gripping the heart of a man, closing the door on one of his pulsing blood-streams, is to find the word acute, or any other word, inadequate. Daddy lay on the couch in our living room, and the lines of pain in his lean face were carved deep and long. His blue eyes, always deeply set, seemed to burn from some far greater depth than I had ever seen before.

The older doctor was out when Mother called, and so his assistant came. He was a young handsome-faced fellow; how soft he seemed against the granite-like contours of my father's face. The young doctor's eyes were large and serious, almost afraid of the terrible intensity of Daddy's voice. "There isn't anything you can give me?" he said. The doctor fumbled in his bag; we had tried the inhalers and all the other pain-erasers that we knew. "I must go for the other doctor," he finally said. "Maybe he is in now. I will find him." So he ran down the steps, relieved, I think, to be away from the incredible penetration of those two blue eyes.

We took Daddy into the bedroom which we had only yesterday moved downstairs. I do not remember anything he said. My eyes and mind and heart seemed to have stood still for the moment, focused with burning alertness on his face and hands and eyes.

The older doctor came, and we did not even realize the swiftness with which he had come. He spoke, and looked at Daddy and turned to his brown leather bag. Then suddenly, with a great gasp upon the air, a great drawing breath of life, my father half moved toward us, and fell back against the waiting pillow. It had been a sound caught winging in mid-air; it had been a half-made, half-completed gesture; it had been a moment.

With a soft cry my mother rushed from the room. The doctor followed her, seeing the terror and loss and stricken grief in her eyes. I could not leave. I stood alone, looking at the bed. Looking at the shape which lay straight and motionless upon it. Now the fears had become reality; now the vague sense of dread which had been born that day in the doctor's office, was brought to the full completed cycle; now the worst had come, and what was there to do?

Fourteen

Within the hour, came the hardest thunder shower of the summer. It came suddenly over the mountains, shaped into dark clouds above the valley, and swept down the hillsides with an avalanche of rain. We were stilled by the force of the storm. We sat in the living room and did not look at one another. The water washed down the window panes, and now and then a crack of thunder reverberated over our heads. Some of the hens had been caught out in the rain, and we could see them huddled under the lilac bush, their feathers soaked and bedraggled. Our crying seemed futile and insignificant against this pouring wetness. We sat alone and thought of the moment of life and the unfathomed strangeness of death. All about us were the mountains and the storm. . . .

As quickly as it had come, the storm left. The sky grew to a grey half-light, and the road and hillside poured streams of water from their sides. In almost no time, we heard a robin in the yard, and the bullfrogs in the pond below. Life gathered itself together and went on, as if the avalanche of rain had never been. We watched with numb eyes and listened with numb ears as the natural world closed around us and carried us on in its inevitable cycle.

MY FATHER had walked in the woods. He had planted pines and flowering shrubs. Once, on the porch, he had pointed out to me the north star which hung over the mountain there beyond us.

In the wintertime after his death, when the trees were bare and the ground was easily visible, we could see the paths which he had made, running along the mountainside, or through the little orchard. And in the next summer, the azaleas and the dogwoods bloomed as beautifully as they ever had. The pines stood evergreen, and the north star shone as clearly, as distant, as it had a year, two thousand years, ago.

To many people I have known, it is a sad thought, a belittling thought, that the woods, sun, planets, paths remain the same when we have left them. It makes them feel that man is somehow made ignoble by the seeming everlastingness of natural forces. I do not feel so. I only feel that man is a part of their everlastingness, that he is a part of the same plan which created these planets and these trees, and that with death he perhaps returns to a fuller, more complete understanding with them than he has ever known on this little world of earth. My father was not saddened or tormented by the feeling of this seeming transiency, this seeming insignificance. He was a part of the fate which was to come to every natural force, and if that fate was tragedy, then tragedy he would accept. He was surrounded by an awareness of what his fate held in common, even if he could not define the answer to that fate. And he made no attempt to suppress these tragic intimations, or shift aside the weights of thought, by taking unto himself the drugging hurry-scurry of the popular mode of living. Banalities to serve as narcotics for the mind he never admitted. There was a singleness of spirit, an essential loneliness, that stood him above the ordinary ways of life and made of him, who was endowed with neither money, social lineage, nor power, a true aristocrat.

On the debit side, I doubt if my father would have accepted some of the changes which have come upon us all so rapidly with the grace my mother met them. It is a difficult thing to watch old beliefs being challenged, and not only meet that challenge but give it your thought, restate the facts to yourself. As he was about his fundamental belief, so my father was about his smaller beliefs. He demanded much of himself and took the burden of much; he expected the same of others. He could not have accepted changes my mother has accepted. She, knowing simple mankind better, knows that as each generation changes, their rules will change. And if there is a rule which remains immutable and inviolable above the common herd of seeking man, then she will believe that it is my father's belief in the oneness of all life.

Mother and my father both looked forward, conceiving of life in its varied forms, encompassing death, passing through its clutches on their mortality as easily as light passes through a window. To my father, death was a fact acknowledged in life, but life was the here and now—it was the small passage of events in the days of a squirrel or a tree or a person. When death came to receive its final acknowledgment, it found, I think, no bitterness or pathos. Instead, my father might have said: "I was as strong as life required, and that was good. Now I shall know some of the answers I have sought. As to a grave, the earth and I were never strangers."

MY FATHER'S LIFE spanned one of the most interesting periods in all of this country's life as a growing young power. The beginning of his life witnessed the tortuous struggle between two sections of his own land, and the close of his life witnessed the first faint steps which were leading toward this present great battle America is waging. From the Civil War, America gained the right to develop freely the vigor of its youth. From this Second World War perhaps America will gain the right to develop freely into the wisdom of its maturity.

My father was a free man in most senses of the word. He was born and raised in a particularly individualistic phase of America's life. It was the era of J. Pierpont Morgan the financier, the manipulator of railroads, of other names bound fabulously with the steel rails running across our continent. Jim Fisk the flashy, Jay Gould, Harriman and Hill, and the little wily Scotsman named Andrew Carnegie. It was the time of the rich sounds of names which burned themselves into a boy's memory and which he would never forget. Chauncey M. Depew, and the Erie railroad. There were unbelievable tales of manipulation and warring factions. There was the Panic of 1873 and the Panic of 1893, with the names of these men, and others, interwoven into a pattern where financial imagination had no limits, where no gamble was too large, where no profit was too unbelievable, and with the public to hold the bag.

Who can describe the pictures of those incredible years as they took place in a boy's life and filled his imagination? What golden inducements did the politics and finances of the country have for a boy whose father was already bound up in the politics of New York state? Many of the men his father brought home were among the most successful politicians of the most powerful state in the Union. They sat at his mother's table in the large old farmhouse and spoke of the destinies of people and parties, of the building of roads and railroads, and of fortunes made and lost with easy grace. These men were filled with a vision of America, they were part and parcel of the industries which were already and which would be in the bright future. And he sat listening, as a boy, and heard the talk of free competition and individualism.

But he also had a vision for America, and for himself. It was not a vision of money and manipulation. How does a boy so young find within himself the determination to break away from the urge for fame? Was it perhaps for this, for an orientation of himself, for a time alone to plan his destiny, that he came to the South the year when he was nineteen? Certainly this place, with the sheep on the grass and with the melancholy wind blowing through the walnut and oak trees which stood around his cabin, was different from the place he had known before. And the reticent, inquisitive mountaineers, oh most certainly they were different from the political friends of his father. Yet he must have found something here for his answer, because there were choices to be made, and he made them in favor of farming, a dairy, and the soil. And who has ever heard of farming being the profession of fame, or dairying the vocation for financial wealth?

In choosing against the world as it had been around him when he was growing up, he could, nevertheless, not revoke completely the romance of those years or the glamour of those names. (Incidentally, this seems to me the most truly glamorous period in all American history, for glamour represents all the material extravagances which were embodied in these years.) I can recall him, when I was small, reading of the lives

Fourteen

. . . .

of the financiers and railroad builders whose names had been so familiar when he was growing up. He always seemed a little amused, a little amazed, at the tangled tale of these people who had spent their whole days in trickery, chicanery, and bargaining and had died in the end the same as he would die, and with no more claim to the earth which would hold them, perhaps not as much claim as he, for he had made friends with the earth and would not find her acquaintance strange.

The influence of individualism remained however, and I do not believe he saw that the new lands for exploration and settlement were becoming less and less, that man was beginning to face a lack of physical expansion. From now on, man would be compelled to turn toward himself for whatever he should need, turn toward his own mind and spirit for adventure and for solution to his problems. This, of course, would have been exactly what my father wanted, this returning to the inner resources. But I wonder if he could see that it was the thinness of these resources that was driving, and would drive, many of the younger people toward any new political faith or art group that might appear on the horizon.

What *have* we found, turning inward as we have been forced to do, especially in the past four years? Has there sprung forth more culture, more sense of the richness of life—or a coated surface of superficial sedatives which can neither quicken our sense of life nor sustain us?

Whatever he saw, or failed to see, appearing on the scene before he left, one quality there was which could encompass them all, the past, the present, the future. That was his belief in America. I do not recall ever hearing him express a wish to visit Europe or England or any of the other foreign countries, as was so fashionable in the twenties, and as we might have done. No, he said, he had not even seen a corner of his own country yet, but he had had proof enough of its beauty in his journey from coast to coast, that he knew he must see America before he saw beyond. At the same time, he realized that to know one section well—its nature, plants, people, atmosphere—was to have some keystone to the rest of the country. He had been fortunate in knowing two small sections, both widely different and yet both of them alike.

I never heard him grow sentimental—sentimentality was almost ridiculously unlike his character—over the American people, as many writers and speakers and laymen are inclined to do. He never believed they were the greatest heroes in history, or the smartest minds, or the most cultured masses, or certainly not the most intelligent people in the art of living. But he believed them to be strong of body with sturdy muscles. He thought of their virtues as: a sense of justice, beneath all the injustice; a sense of humor, beneath all their determination to "get somewhere"; a tolerance of race and creed and ideas, in spite of all the intolerance they had borne. Justice, humor, tolerance, and added to that a sort of glorious esprit de corps, shall we call it, which, when it needed to, could plunge so much of fancy and resource into a new fad of hair-cutting, or into a battle for all the freedoms which it believed were being challenged.

My father never fought in any of America's battles. He never gained a fortune and endowed some national library or gallery. But when it came time to vote, he considered all the facts he could gather in the matter, and voted for the people he believed finest. No popular pressure could swerve him in his choice, once made. He treated those who worked for him with respect and dignity and gave them more pay than they asked, when their work deserved it. The different mountain boys who worked for him around our place, when I was small, listened to him because he was older than they and spoke for their good, respected him because he respected them, and would have done almost anything he asked because he was fair with them. Mountaineers appreciate fairness probably above all other qualities. Then, my father was thoughtful. Perhaps he was one in a long evolving cycle of common men who think and feel and are aware of the world around them, and who will someday change the course of

....

the world. He read what men had written in books and papers, and what the great spirit or force had written in the land and growing things. And somehow, he himself was made a reconciler between the two, one of many who are quiet and strong, going their way with imagination and feeling toward a harmony of all life.

NOW I KNEW that I would go away. Now I knew that all this which had gone before me was simply prelude, and that it was a prelude ended. Stilled forever. I had crawled and skipped and run and leaped and wondered and cried and sung through the prelude. Now the last chord was struck and the cadence was completed. Everything to come hereafter would be another movement, building toward another climax. I wanted to stand back and look at the beginning and the following. I held myself still and tried to feel back into the moments I had known. But even as I turned and held a hand to the feeling, I was rushing on into the future. There was no end without beginning, and life was a circle which found beginning or ending anywhere, but never any break.

I had been happy beside the creek called Beaverdam. Yet, even while I was there, I was forever leaving. My father and my mother had been happy there in every day, because it was an end and a completion for each of them. But I was different, and for me, it was a beginning and could be no more, no less. It was tomorrow toward which I leaned; it was the city toward which I looked. Could I have known then that once gone I would never return to the valley or the mountains, the crawfish or the wild dewberries, and find them as once they were; could I have known then that those symbols, things, and people whom I loved there would never be the same again, but cast into a harsh perspective—knowing these things, would I then have spent my dreams and energies quite differently?

I think not. For we are each what we are, and there is no path set for any one of us by which he may with certainty find a single glimmer of the light he struggles after. But lacking paths and finding few returns still, who is there among us who can say he has lived upon this earth, in his own time, and never once been blinded by the clear light of beauty in that splinter of immortal splendor which is man and plant and animal, and life in all its forms? Certainly not I.